To Lori —

Many happy
hours of reading
pleasure await
you!

Love,
Suzanne

# BEGINNER'S GUIDE TO TROPICAL FISH AND FISH TANKS

# BEGINNER'S GUIDE TO TROPICAL FISH AND FISH TANKS

Reginald Dutta BA FZS

Illustrations by Olive Dutta

Pelham Books

First published in Great Britain by
PELHAM BOOKS LTD
52 Bedford Square
London, W.C.1
JUNE 1971
SECOND IMPRESSION OCTOBER 1971

© 1971 by Reginald Dutta

7207 0472 3

Printed lithographically in Great Britain
by Hollen Street Press Ltd, at Slough
and bound by James Burn at Esher, Surrey

To the Staff, Fish, and Customers of
Fish Tanks Ltd., without whose co-operation
this knowledge might never have been gained.
Fish Tanks Ltd., 49 Blandford Street, London, W.1.

# Contents

# CONTENTS

# Illustrations

*The author and the publishers gratefully acknow-
ledge permission to use the photographs of
Laurence E. Perkins*

# CHAPTER ONE

# IT'S THE FISH THAT COUNTS

Let's get first things right first. Who is the most important one concerned with the fish tank? Clearly it's not you. It's the fish. For the fish the tank is its whole home and its whole life, twenty-four hours of each and every day, no change, no holiday, no escape. Only a heartless selfish brute could fail to register that, on reflection; a kindly human would cease at once such talk as 'it's only to amuse the kids, or just to fill in that space' – who but a cruel tyrant would sacrifice fish life and happiness 'just to amuse someone or to fulfil some whim'!

So, it's the fish that counts.

Fortunately fish are very accommodating creatures and are only too anxious to co-operate, to please, to take on your habits and to do all they can to make you glad. They just ask to live, decently if possible; happily if also possible; then they will offer you years of friendship and adoration in return, they will come when you call or when you approach the fish tank; they will listen to your voice, flapping excited fins in response, all to a degree that you just won't believe till you've had your own fish tank for a month or so and have personally verified these truths.

And if you now think that fish have no feelings, have no psychic rapport with you, can't hear your voice or feel your presence, then they'll soon teach you the contrary. That's why they make such good pets. Added to which they demand very little of your time or attention in return *provided* that you have set up their home with knowledge and skill, as well as understanding; in other words, that you have bought your tank from a specialist dealer who really knows his job and can put you on the right lines from the word go. A 'pet shop' dealer has little hope of keeping abreast with this rapidly changing, fast-growing industry if his attention is spread over dogs, cats or whatever – he *has* to concentrate only and solely on fish; a general knowledge of mammals is no more applicable to tropical fish than is a general knowledge of clothes to choosing an expensive fur coat, or a general knowledge of motor-cars is applicable to making an orbiting missile. You need a specialist, a true expert, one who gives all his time, energy and resources to fish alone.

# CHAPTER TWO

# CREATING A HOME
# FIT FOR THE FISH

Again, first things first – the home should be big enough;
fish suffer and die in cramped conditions just like you and
I would. So please get the very largest tank that is
practicable. Other furnishings and fittings can always be
added later, as and when possible; but, once bought, the
tank can't be enlarged. The air surface of the prospective
new tank is the real key, rather than mere volume of water,
as its area controls the rate at which the good gases like
oxygen can come into the water and the bad gases like
carbon dioxide can escape out. Fouling, decay, smells and
disease become increasingly liable as the area of the air
surface becomes smaller; beware of the plausible dealer
who says it will be all right if you have air bubbles from
a small pump; these bubbles will certainly help, but will
they help enough! Tanks with a small air surface usually
need sophisticated filters that probably cost as much as the
money 'saved' by getting a tank whose air surface was too
small.

Specialist tanks are constantly coming into the shops for
sale and many are most beautiful and original in design;
but they should all conform to Mother Nature's basic law
of an ample air surface, and the customer who ignores this
gets the troubles he deserves, not to mention the poor fish
who suffer and die.

Fabulous is about the only word to describe the choice
of tanks now available. Still going strong are the light-
weights pressed steel frames glazed with thin glass; cheap

to buy and quick to leak the public loves them and they are sold in thousands of pet shops over five continents. At one time it looked as though the trouble with leaks would finally cause them to be replaced by better versions but improved sealing glues have prolonged their usefulness, and many a small child has pestered many a harassed parent into buying one – as it is so cheap.

The more robust, more reliable, strong angle-iron framed tank also continues as a firm favourite. Again, very inexpensive, it too is widely sold and looks like so continuing for decades to come. It used to rust, but the nylon coatings, and polythene coatings of the angle-iron have cured that. It used to leak, especially if emptied and moved, but the new liquid rubber sealers have cured that too. It's a good old familiar friend, and deserves to be.

These new liquid rubberised sealers are an important technical break-through. Before their advent the angle-iron had to be wide enough to allow sufficient waterproofing; dealers used to (and still do) skimp on this width resulting in greater leaks but in cheaper tanks; now the new sealers will join glass to glass, eliminating the angle-iron altogether if required. Thus have grown up a whole generation of new type tanks : on the one hand all-glass completely frameless versions; on the other, many lovely metals previously not robust enough to allow adequate sealing but now being increasingly used – stainless steel, plastic strips and anodised aluminium to mention but three. More and more popular is becoming the custom of mixing materials in previously unheard of combinations : glass with wood, with plastics and resins of all kinds, as well as with metals. Such tanks can be very very beautiful and original; or even just be cheap and functional.

Of course, the biggest single change has come from the plastic industry as this now gears up to stamp out in-one-unbroken-piece tanks of useful depths and widths; years ago, a few inches was all the depth that was readily available, but as that has changed a stream of specialist plastic tanks descends on a delighted public which cannot but help marvel at the originality, variety, beauty, and colours of this fascinating new media. Especially the colours. Plastics have the endearing quality of catching the light and of allowing it to travel through their slightly etherical form, to give intriguing and ever-changing hues. Add to colour two other big advantages of plastics, namely curves and fluting; these can be designed to give works of sheer beauty quite impossible with the more rigid and older-fashioned materials. And, to top it all, plastic tanks are light in weight – an important point in these modern days of air travel.

Rectangular tanks to go along a wall, on a shelf or a table; triangular ones to fit snugly into a corner though at the serious sacrifice of air-surface and hence of fish capacity; square or multi-sided ones that you can walk right round, can incorporate into a decor for your table or for circular seating; tanks encased in wood or in plastic cabinets, rather like T.V. sets; bowl-shaped tanks in single or in multiple units, with or without decorative stands; tanks with sloping fronts, sloping sides, coming forward or receding back; curved fronts, convex or concave; combinations of all these – fantastic choices, all of which we have made or sold here in the heart of London's West End. We love to make a truly one-off job, the only single one in existence, just specially for that spot in that room, in that decor, in that shape, in that exact finish; to look gorgeous!

If you have a boat or a yacht and you want tanks to house decorative (or even edible) fish, we can do so quite easily. Long since solved are design difficulties of equalising pressures and partial vacuum as the ship pitches and rolls, and the tank water surges and falls.

More humdrum but very useful tanks for breeding, for isolation; tanks divided into two or more parts; all now are readily available from your specialist dealer. The pet shop man might have just sold you a 'tank divider', often a piece of plastic inserted snugly into the tank to separate one portion from another, and have let it go at that; a specialist dealer would probably have warned you that perforating the plastic may not ensure an even distribution of heat in the separated parts, and may thus have saved you many a future (unnecessary) headache.

*Tank position*

Now that you have bought your (big an air surface as possible) tank, where are you going to position it? Too much light, especially sunlight, means that the water will tend to grow green unless you have truly adequate filters, which are fortunately readily available. Too many fumes from a kitchen and a bathroom for example would also call for a change of site, or a filter. Too near a window would tend to induce greater temperature fluctuations as the outside climate changes, and would call for a stronger heating unit. Padding, between the tank and the window glass, would be a sensible precaution. Even a simple piece of hardboard would help, and would also cut out excess light if it were higher and longer than the tank itself.

Then, where are you going to sit? You may now think this is a silly question, but when you have become entranced by your tank, a powerfully riveting focus for you and your friends, you'll find yourself shifting furniture around so that you can sit the more frontally and nearer the tank! If circumstances force you to remain far away, then have fewer bigger fish in a bigger tank, rather than numerous small ones not so readily viewed from a distance, to save your constantly going over to peer at the fascinating colours and antics.

To save constant backache and osteopath fees, please put the tank at a sensible height off the ground. Ideally, its BASE should be 36 in. up from the floor for sitting eye-level, and 48 in. for places like a hall-way or corridor where you are normally standing or walking. Tropical fish especially, lose far too much of their beauty if looked at from above; they should be at eye-level, or above. This point is important, and is not always realised at the beginning; many a lovely tank has been placed too low down 'because the furniture is modern' or the architect said so, and then has had to be raised to eye level again.

*Stands*

When full of water, sand and the decorative rocks the tank can be heavy, so that any stand needs to be robust. As a rough guide an 18 in. x 12 in. x 12 in. filled tank would weigh ¾ cwt, a 24 in. x 12 in. x 12 in, about ¾ and 1 cwt, and a 36 in. x 12 in. x 12 in. 2 cwt; although these are static weights, there is no jolting or movement, and are evenly distributed over the tank base area, so they are not quite as frightening as they first appear.

To repeat, other trends notwithstanding, the ideal height of the stand for sitting eye level is 36 in. for optimum fish beauty, and 48 in. for standing viewing.

Many and various are the types available. The dear old metal angle-iron one is still deservedly popular because it is functional and very cheap, often it has a second metal frame support lower down which can house an additional tank or hold simply a glass shelf for ornaments, etc. Really beautiful wrought-iron decorations, incorporating the second tank and/or assorted shelves at differing heights and sizes to hold books, flowers, concealed lights, and so on, are widely available – again at very reasonable cost. The bookcase stand is a standard sales item for example. If the legs of the stands are being made especially slim for better effect, it can help to splay them forwards or sideways for greater stability. Skirting boards can easily be accommodated by making a suitable kink in the leg, say 8 in. up from the floor, and so saving space by not having the stand projecting out from the wall an unnecessary 2 in.

To help the poor old dealer save storage space, knock-down versions are increasingly being marketed and are a real boon to the mail-order customer, as well as to carry-it-away yourself types. Ever tried to pack a 36 in. x 12 in. x 36 in. stand into the back of a family car together with the Saturday shopping, the kids home from school, and the squashable groceries?

Tanks can be hung from the ceiling, be put on (as well as in) the wall with brackets; be housed on tall fluted wood columns, singly or in multiple columns, often in a trio of a tall central column flanked by two shorter and more slender ones, interlaced or not according to taste.

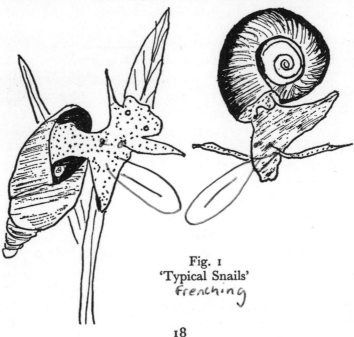

Fig. 1
'Typical Snails'
Frenching

CHAPTER THREE

# HEATING THE HOME
# FIT FOR THE FISH

In these days of an affluent society, tropical fish ask for their share of central heating too; for some of us humans it's a welcome, or unobtainable luxury, but for the fish it is literally a matter of life or death. Most tropicals have a wide temperature tolerance but an ideal of 72°–80°F. (23°–27°C.) is best for long lived health. Of course, they can go down to 45°F. (7°C.) for relatively short periods of a few hours although they can drear on in lethargic misery at 68°F. (20°C.) for months or more, but that's just like taking a man from the equator and making him live in the arctic snows, unless he grumbled enough to make you do something about it. Similarly, at the other extreme fish wilt at 95°F. or more (35°C.) as the increased temperature automatically lowers the oxygen content of the water. Again, they can survive, especially with aeration, but tend to weaken.

However, these rules are not as hard and fast as they were once, mostly because of air travel. In the old days fish were bred locally, say in the same continent, but now they are regularly imported from hitherto quite inaccessible regions deep in forests, swamps, a thousand miles or more up river in shallow streams, dense in the jungle. The local temperatures are often 90°–110°F. in the shade, and fish make the air journey to your dealer in one day! No wonder they need to be acclimatized. Chocolate Gourami are typical of such fish, coming from the swampy interior of Malaysia and thriving at 95°F. (35°C.) they deteriorate rapidly unless very carefully accustomed to lower temperatures. And they are such lovely fish, who have been given a bad name of being weak mostly because of cold.

Two golden rules for all and especially for those in Europe or America :

(1) for sustained temperatures of over 80°F. (27°C.) aeration and/or filters are particularly helpful, the higher the temperature the greater the water circulation required to offset the lowered oxygen content of the water and the subsequent increased danger of fouling.

(2) the whole tank has to be heated; particularly the very bottom one inch where the catfish rest. If there are stratified layers or areas of hot and cold then the fish suffer as you and I would if continually forced to leave a warm room, go out into the cold, return, go out again, and so on. Hence the heater should be placed horizontally right down in the very very lowest inch of the tank and heat right through from below up. Water circulation sufficient to diffuse the heat evenly should be maintained either by aeration or by an adequate number of fish, numerous and active enough to ensure this. This stratification of the water will explain many a mysterious 'going off their food' or 'growing listless', and particularly applies to some of the more exotically designed tanks that have 'out-lying areas' of water far from the heater, with weak water circulation.

Climatic conditions govern the strength of the heater required to maintain the optimum 72°–80°F. (23°–27°C.), as does the local situation of the tank – draughts or abutting right up to a window (see page 16) can make heavy calls on the heater especially in the 2 a.m. to 4 a.m. period when the ambient temperature is at its lowest. But we give below the strengths for London and for southern England that experience has proved best.

18 in. x 10 in. x 10 in. tank    75 watts (100 in cold site)
18 in. x 12 in. x 12 in. tank   100 watts (125 in cold site)
24 in. x 12 in. x 12 in. tank   125 watts (150 in cold site)
36 in. x 12 in. x 12 in. tank   200 watts (250 in cold site)
48 in. x 12 in. x 12 in. tank   300 watts (375 in cold site)

In tanks of 36 in. x 12 in. x 12 in. we tend to put two heaters of 100 or 125 watts each, rather than one of a bigger wattage; partly because of more even heat distribution, partly because of cost, and partly because of reliability and replacement ease. But the heater has to be right down in the very bottom one inch of the tank, as already stressed, and the tank decor discussed later in Chapter 8 will allow for this.

Making the heater unnecessarily strong merely throws an unfair burden on the thermostat which wears out quicker, sticks, and boils your fish. If you wish to be ultra-cautious then put the additional heater on a separate thermostat of its own. Our experience here at Fish Tanks Ltd., of selling hundreds upon thousands of tanks over the decades have more than justified the reliability and long service of the above recommended strengths for rectangular shaped tanks; speciality tanks with curving arms, sweeping areas, outlying limbs, etc., are in a class by themselves and need a specialist dealer to guide you.

Heaters are usually sold in varying strengths; we keep them at 25w, 40w, 50w, 60w, 75w, 100w, 125w and 150w with a few stronger ones for special jobs. The good old type of a pyrex glass test-tube, with the heating coil would round an inner core, is still the unbeatable favourite, having lasted since pre-war days! It is quite a record.

One rather important point to watch and one that not every pet shop dealer will be able to satisfy is that the flex from the heater should be really long enough. Consider that the flex has to travel inconspicuously down the corner of the tank; right, but right to the very very bottom;

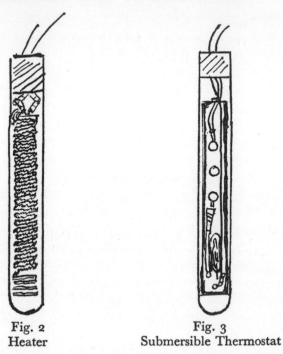

Fig. 2
Heater

Fig. 3
Submersible Thermostat

along the bottom (buried out of sight) under the sand to the optimum spot from the point of decor (see Chapter 8) and of heat distribution, and you may come to rue the day your heater flex is too short and you have the darn thing hanging in full view with the vital bottom inch of your tank cold, and your catfish ill.

Of course the pyrex test tube is being challenged by magnetic strip heaters, metal heaters, extra-long, extra-slim (and extra easy to break) heaters, by unbreakable plastic heaters (a strong contender), flexible rubber-covered wires to bury under the sand, etc., etc. However, whatever your taste and your tank, there will certainly be a suitable heater readily available.

The thermostat to control the heater and to switch it

on/off within a set range has also survived basically un-altered since pre-war days, and by now must have been sold literally in millions. It, too, is the good old pyrex glass test-tube housing a bi-metallic strip which bends unevenly with temperature change to make and break contact, and so to switch the heater on and off. Simple, functional, efficient.

Refinements galore have come, and most have gone. A neon light incorporated to show when the heater is on (or off) is a popular improvement. So, too, are heavier-duty ones to switch the aerator and even the tank's top lighting on and off with the heat. This applies mostly to tanks that are left unattended for long periods while the family are on holiday, or for other particularised uses like breeding. Many have been, and are, the attempts to combine the heater with the thermostat, in spite of the obvious disadvantages of housing the heater directly with the thermostat, and of the rather bulky unit so produced. Fully submersible thermostats still out-sell those with external adjustment knobs (which get accidentally knocked or twiddled with by well meaning friends). The same applies to external thermostats that stick on to the outside of the tank glass – protective caps and push-guards over the knobs notwithstanding.

Like the heaters, and the tanks, the choice is fabulous; you would indeed be fussy not to find just what you needed, easily and cheaply.

With thermometers, too, the choice is as great. Legibility of the figures is important, especially as the instrument is usually hidden out of sight, and so too are their durability as some rub off or fade in use. Circular stick-on thermometers are beginning to replace the more usual glass tubular mercury or even spirit columns, as their bi-metallic spring loading principle has been found to be neat and reliable. A useful tip is to place at twelve-o'clock-high the favourite temperature you want, say 78°F., so that the circular thermometer needle is vertical; any deviation from vertical will readily indicate the temperature change without you having to peer at the figures. Useful, too, is to place the thermometer half-way up the height of the tank : hot water rises, so that a thermometer placed high up or low down tends to give unnecessarily false readings, especially if the water circulation is insufficient and temperature stratification exists.

All parts of the heating unit, the heater, the thermostat and the thermometer, are functional rather than decorative and should be housed strictly out of sight. We just would not allow them to be seen or heard. Chapter 8 on decor gives tips on how the rocks, plants and ornaments can be arranged to achieve this. Little plastic (and other materials) holders to clip the glass tubes into chosen areas and angles are helpful accessories, so too are multi-unit 'junction boxes' neatly to connect the leads from the various electrical necessities and to get rid of that mass of tangled wires. Your specialist dealer would do all this for you normally. Better ones have a service where they will come to your home to install the tank, or, at least, to do the wiring for you in the shop so that you have only to plug in when you get home.

# CHAPTER FOUR

# AIR CONDITIONING THE HOME FIT FOR THE FISH

*Aerators and Filters*

In several very widely-sold earlier books air pumps have been played down by me because as they were then the pumps were noisy – or dear – and a tank 'balanced' without aeration was normal. It still is, and quite half the tanks we sell have no aerators or filters and keep clear and healthy in gruelling conditions. But two factors have caused a change towards the end of the 1960–70 decade : a real technical break-through, and a rising standard of living which makes the public more ready to buy what were formerly optional extras. In America aeration has been a 'must' for a long long time, but not in Europe – until towards the end of the 1960–70 period.

The technical break-through has been two-fold : the Americans with the magnetic coil, and the Germans with the water cooled unit; both of which give a pump that really is silent, really will run day and night without overheating, really has enough strength, and is not unduly expensive. Other nations, including the English and the Japanese have noted and have copied. Aerators and filters are now rapidly approaching the status of a standard fitting. A third factor has been the marked improvement in the old-established vibrator air pumps. These have always been cheap, and became increasingly noisy as the 'rubber bellows' inside them were worn out and pumped vibration rather than air. Newer versions with lateral bellows replacing the older vertical ones, using better 'rub-

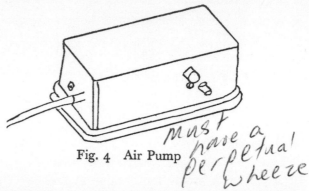

Fig. 4   Air Pump *must have a perpetual wheeze*

ber' substitutes, longer lasting and more and more powerful, have transformed the pumps radically. The claims of their makers for 'silent' and even for 'strong' have a meaning now that a sceptical public would have denied in earlier days. And they were still cheap.

So aeration has firmly come to stay, and the choice available is again fabulous. Refinements like bleed-off valves to ease back-pressure, like air-volume control knobs, like replacement 'bellows' for the vibrators, are all common, and the customer usually has umpteen makes and some five nationalities to pick from at prices ranging from schoolboy to millionaire; mostly schoolboy.

As a direct result several improvements have ensued :

(1) Perhaps most important of all, at long long long last you can now keep a tank in a bright spot without getting pestered by that filthy slimy clinging clogging green algae! Remember the stuff! Who hasn't been plagued by it? Algae grows very fast under strong lights, including sunlight, and used to overrun the tank; it still grows in such conditions but the filters powered by the new pumps can easily cope with its rate of reproduction and maintain the tank clean and clear. A really big advance. Now you can house your beautiful, decorative, richly planted fish tank in your sun lounge, shop windows; big-windowed

showroom, entrance hall or boardroom; an open air arcade, garden-walk; amid arc lights, spot lights or whatever.

But the old golden rules still apply, and your airpump and filter must be big enough for the job. You would not expect to power an aircraft carrier with the outboard motor of a dingy, and the rule is still true that when a filter gets clogged up and saturated it tends to cease work and worse still to pump back foul poisoned water. You need to clean it, and the frequency of the cleaning depends on the size of the filter and its ratio to the work. Sunlight, for instance, is usually measured in millions of candle-power, so beware of too small a filter.

(2) You can now keep more fish with a given air-surface of water than before; improved water circulation from filters, as distinct from air bubbles from a diffuser stone, give quicker absorption of oxygen into the water and faster elimination of noxious gases and particles. The golden rule for fish capacity of tropicals of average length of $1\frac{1}{4}$ in. was :

| | | |
|---|---|---|
| 18 in. x 12 in. air surface | – | 18–20 fish |
| 24 in. x 12 in. air surface | – | 24–28 fish |
| 36 in. x 12 in. air surface | – | 36–40 fish |
| 48 in. x 12 in. air surface | – | 48–54 fish |

Old type aeration increased this by 40 per cent; the new power filters can lift the increase to up 60–70 per cent; but you mustn't cheat – *power* filters are meant, not just aeration.

(3) With increased water circulation are eliminated problems of temperature differences in layers as stratification disappears, including the vital one inch at the bottom.

(4) From a design point of view greater freedom in the shape of the tank means more original shapes and forms. The golden rule of air surface holds true, of course, but rapid circulation means ever-changing surface and greater

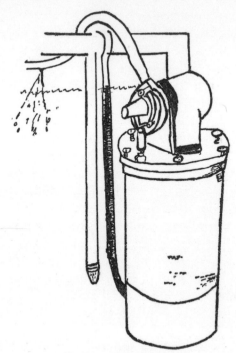

Fig. 5    Power Filter

absorption as the whole volume of flowing water is constantly brought into play.

(5) In natural life fish are often accustomed to running
streams, with their eddies and surges; now these can all be
reproduced in your fish tank by a luxurious combination
of a power filter, an under gravel filter and aeration. This
triple unit really is luxury, but repays its cost in fish health
and fascination. For example, why waste the power of the
returning stream water? Let it fall from half an inch above
water and trap myriad dancing air bubbles to frolic
through the water. Let it sweep across the air surface
almost horizontally to clear off any top scum that would
normally increase 'surface tension' of the water and so

inhibit the oxygen absorption rate, not to mention fouling the fish food in its oily scum. Let it jet deep into the heart of the tank to flush out dusty corners, or to bounce off a chosen rock so as to wave and sway some graceful plants, or even to power the rotation of an ornamental wheel or windmill. There are so many lovely uses, and all help the health and joy of the fish, who will respond and play all the more. There are many fish like the zebra Danios that delight in 'fighting their way upstream' and repeatedly will 'dive' into the jet of water and play and surf ride, and helter-skelter downstream in gales of fish laughter.

*Types of Filters*

The good old box filter with a layer of activated carbon and white wool to trap the loose floating particles is still going strong and is still the most popular. Of course, there

Fig. 6  Hand Pump        Fig. 7  Hand Pump with Bag

Fig. 8   Undergravel Filter

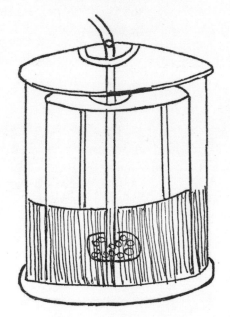

Fig. 9   Airstream Filter

have been improvements. The activated charcoal is far more effective in absorbing hostile bacteria, noxious gases, fish urine (a very important factor, too often overlooked) than before; the horrible glass-wool that splintered in your hand has long since passed into the museum archives, and the latest plastic-based 'wools' have completely taken over.

In the design of the box filter itself two main developments have come to stay. The base of the box has been removed (or perforated) to allow suction up direct from the sand covering the tank bottom, and thus giving a far wider field of cleaning; limited only by the strength of the air pump causing the suction. Secondly, the air stream from the pump now often is diverted into an auxiliary chamber to give a most pleasing and beautiful effect of dancing air bubbles, as well as the normal cleaning suction.

Also entrenching itself is the under-gravel filter, in which the dirt is collected out of sight but is none the less ever-present, in the filter buried under the tank sand. Everything looks clean, but the dirt is still there; merely it has been 'swept under the carpet'. But the public insist on buying these under-gravel filters, which have responded by improved surface area, improved water circulation, and, hence of improved efficiency. Like them or not, they are obviously here to stay.

By far and away the most efficient filters are the containers external to the tank and powered by the water-cooled pumps especially, and by the magnetic-coiled circulating ones. By having the filter chamber quite separate and outside the tank you can get one truly big enough and really capable of heavy duty work. Many will last a whole year without cleaning and, incredible as it may seem, run constantly that whole time without over-heating or attention. It really is wonderful. One important point to watch though, especially for the water cooled ones – do not let the water syphon break; when started these

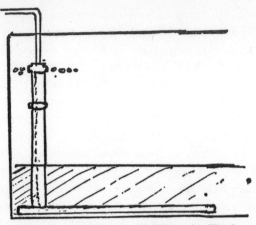

Fig. 10   Under-gravel Filter in Tank

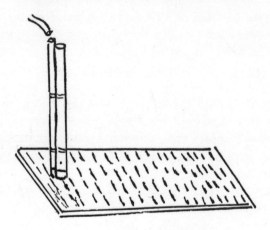

Fig. 11   Under-gravel Filter

pumps have to be 'primed' i.e. the pump container, the inlet tube and the outlet tube have all to be completely full of water, free of air bubbles, so that the water circulates freely; if this water circulation is broken, say by the inlet tube coming out of the tank water, then the pump rapidly empties itself (no new water coming into it from the inlet

Rosy Barbs

Tiger Barbs

Black Widow

Dwarf Gourami

tube) and overheats through lack of water. Other than that the filter is flawless.

Neat refinements continually come forth for many models like 'easy-pack' carbon replacements, disposable cartridges to save cleaning or washing out; granular chemicals mixed in with the glass wool so making the activated carbon unnecessary; neat cradles to hold the external filters so that they can be hung on to the tank sides or rear, if there is no shelf nearby. Filters should all be kept at tank water level and not housed above or below. This can be a bore, but it still is an essential precaution.

## Ozoniser

The very latest in cleanliness technique, a sort of aquarist's space gun which emits $O_3$ instead of the conventional oxygen $O_2$ and whose extra-concentration kills bacteria. Because relatively small dosages can be lethal to fish it is usual to play the ozoniser on to the filter, from which the flow then goes to the tank. If no such buffer as the filter is possible then it may help to play the ozoniser $O_3$ stream on to a rock from which the stream bounces off, diffused rather than concentrated.

A most useful accessory, at present somewhat rare and somewhat expensive, it is certain to grow more popular. By it the sterilisation of a tank can be done easily in minutes, rather than the old-fashioned clean and boil and scrub techniques. Periodic short doses are favoured by some, rather than a steady extra-low permanent stream.

Apart from the danger to the fish, this $O_3$ stream kills the helpful as well as the hostile bacteria, and its use obviously demands care.

# CHAPTER FIVE

# LIGHTING THE HOME
# FIT FOR THE FISH

The simple things of older days still survive – one electric bulb of 25 watts per square foot of air surface and per 12 in. of water depth held 2 in. above water surface; for decades this has done great service, and so continues now. Usually the bulbs are housed in a metal cover fitting snugly all-over the tank top keeping in the fish, and keeping out dust, cats and small children; unobtrusive drip flanges feed back the condensation into the tank, so reducing evaporation especially if the air temperature of the room is colder than that of the tropical tank itself – a situation that encourages rapid water evaporation. Nice little air vents in the side of the metal cover just sufficient for ventilation, but not enough to accelerate evaporation are also fitted. It was, and is, functional, efficient and cheap; it was, and is, popular.

Kept on for eight hours a day in a normal room this system grows the plants nicely without letting the green slimy algae become too obvious, and gives a pleasant all-over diffused light restful to the human eye. Darker rooms like basements could do with eight to ten hours per day, and brighter ones with sunlight present could be reduced right down to four hours, depending on how the plants thrived and the algae didn't. Too much light produces excess algae; the bulbs may be too strong, they may be lit for too long, or the room could be too bright, in which case the tank could be re-sited in a darker spot, or be shaded from the natural daylight, e.g. by some books, a photograph, etc., something large enough to throw sufficient shadow; or have a filter fitted as described in Chapter 4.

The bulbs are easy to replace (with one of the same strength of only 25 watts), but if they blow too often the cause is nearly always because the tank is not sitting level but is sloping backwards. Perhaps the floor or the table, etc., on which it sits is slightly sloped or uneven. Instead of dropping forward into the tank the water condensation then tends to seep backwards to the electric bulbs and blow them. A simple cure is to raise the metal cover fractionally at the rear, even $\frac{1}{16}$ of an inch, or jamming a matchstick between it and the tank top would do, so that the condensation flows forward again.

Some people like to have feeding holes cut into the all-over metal covers, to which we always fit sliding metal discs to keep the holes closed when not in actual use in order to inhibit water evaporation.

Other people prefer the cover to stop short some four or six inches from the front of the tank and to have a hinged flap for easier feeding and maintenance. This can be very useful unless the flap is too wide in proportion to the cover so that the light is on the rear part of the tank mostly, leaving the front in shadow. Should this happen we like to fit auxiliary lighting to restore the plant growth, sometimes a spot-light, or all manner of helpful variations as will be described below.

For most people the covers are so light and pliable, usually made of rustless aluminium, that feeding holes and hinged flaps are superfluous.

Plastic is beginning to replace aluminium as the basic material for the cover. Stamped out in great numbers for standardised sizes these plastic covers are amazingly low in price. They have, too, the endearing quality of all plastics of 'letting light travel' through them to give a warm glowing-all-over effect that is definitely attractive.

Fluorescent tubes and striplights have never competed successfully with the more usual ordinary household light bulb, speciality uses of restricted space apart, but the 'Gro-lux' type of American lighting has begun a massive invasion since the end of the nineteen sixties. In essence this 'Gro-lux' cuts out the 'yellowish' caste given by the household bulb and highlights the blues, reds, greens, etc., of the fish and plant colours; the light is 'gin clear', and certainly enhances most fish. Delicate hues that were often 'lost' in the yellow caste are brought right out, and the public have understandably fallen for it in a big way. It is more expensive, and more complicated to fit, but its well worth it. We supply wiring diagrams with our do-it-yourself kits and many people seem to cope quite happily. For the more-busy or the less-practical you can always call on the specialist dealer to do it for you.

Many indeed are the most beautiful variations that can be done, to please both the fish and the customer. In their natural habitats both are accustomed to changing lights, of varying intensities and angles: for the fish there is not only the change from dawn – noon – dusk, but every varying foliage and vegetation and changing water depths, all of which mean fluctuations and variety. For the customer there is the bright glare of the cocktail party or the hushed peace of the headache, so both like alternative lighting in the fish tank. At dusk, or in other subdued light, it is extraordinarily soothing and relaxing to sit with only the light of the fish tank, calmly radiating; then as the dusk deepens to night, try switching off the (relatively bright) top lighting of the tank and put on the even softer diffused auxiliary rear-lighting that gently glows through the whole width of the placid waters of your tank. Tensions ease out, insomnia and worries just melt, replaced by a gentle yet living silence. Often we paint the rear of the tank in a lovely soft colour, thickened here and there, to silhouette a 'line of distant mountains', and the rear light shining back to you through this 'view', fronted by the waters of your fish tank, just joyous. Effective only in soft light and in gentle moods, it is something we love to make.

Another version is to have secondary lighting concealed in the tank stand, especially if this is a decorative one housing plants, ornaments, and so on. Gayer and very stimulating tank versions have an automatic on/off sequence usually in a run of three – on, a bright white light; off, to a subdued light and then back to the original white light to re-start the sequence. The pauses between changes are quite dramatic, as is the total presentation. A further very pleasant variation on this triple sequence is to have two with diffused light (say a coloured and a white) and the third with an intensely focused light which sends a single narrow shaft to one chosen spot only in the tank. At this spot we put a strong motif, a reflective metal, a moving part like a wheel or a dancing air stream, a waving plant, a floating strip of featured plastic – all manner of delightful touches, so easy for you to express yourself and your mood. And, of course, the fish love it too.

Naturally, there are fundamental rules imposed by Mother Nature which a wise man obeys. The nearer you sit to the tank, the more focused can be your light; at the far end of the room soft diffusion is more harmonious. Again, too intense a focus for too long will invite algae, so direct the light beam on to a substance that is inhibiting to algae, such as metals, resins and crystals. The ratio of over-all light to the room should not be too great, or the pleasant focus turns into a glaring hypnotic distraction. And, above all, the balance of the tank must be maintained – the plants and the fish must be happy too; as indeed they are intermingled with areas of shade and light, of brilliant shafts and streaky glens or crevices, so that they too can choose according to their mood of the moment.

In truth much happiness can be had by all; just give us a free hand to design your fish tank.

# CHAPTER SIX

# FURNISHING THE
# HOME FIT FOR
# THE FISH

Artistry, love and understanding for the fish, skill in execution of design, practical rules ensuring long service, these are among the truths that soon begin to differentiate between the pet shop man and the specialist dealer; a sensitive awareness is more important than crude flash, and the next three chapters seek to illustrate this, to help to achieve this.

Having got a big enough tank, with a big enough air surface (or power filter), nicely positioned, warmed and lit, we can now set about making the interior look gorgeous, creating the aquascape in fact.

Let us start with the sand at the base of the tank. It needs to be fine enough for the fish to pick up in their mouths, to swill round, to forage into, to dig into, to rub against, to hollow out, to lay eggs in, to pick up and to blow against rocks so cleaning their surface and preparing them for adhesive eggs; in short, it has to be fine enough! But not so fine that it will matt down preventing all this happy activity, choking the plants as their roots are restricted from spreading easily. Nor, too, must it be too coarse, again preventing the above everyday activities and entrapping particles of food that lie and rot between its wide crevices. It has to be just right; it should be a lovely golden colour. No wonder we bring ours all the way from the Channel Islands into the heart of London's West End, and sell it by the ton.

Love of colour, and fear of oil pollution has activated

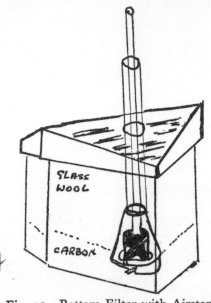

*But, it must* (handwritten)

Fig. 12   Bottom Filter with Airstone

*buzz all nite if you have a roommate* (handwritten)

the sales of 'artificial sands' made of an ever widening circle of materials, starting with crushed stones, crushed coral, and believe it or not dyed cork which finally sinks when saturated and 'treated'. Yellow, white, black, green, red, and blue, mixed or pure; in streaks, in patterns, in squares; dividing the tank floor laterally, horizontally; accentuating this, focusing away from/to/by/in that; all sorts of gay fun is yours for the enterprise. But Mother Nature still rules: the darker the tank floor (at least in suitable patches) the better the colours of the fish and the more restful to the catfish, and the consistency must be of the Channel Island natural sand described above. Finally, it must be, positively, non-toxic to fish, all dyes being fast, for example.

Not everyone seems to realise that rocks dissolve appreciably in water, altering what is technically known as 'the total dissolved solids' and so harming the fish. Many a gradual listless decline and death has its origin here quite unsuspected. That weather beaten, full of holes and worn shapes, Westmorland rock is very nice to behold, but is a pernicious death-trap since it dissolves far too readily. The 'hard' stones, free of lime, awkward to mine, difficult to break into attractive pieces are the ones Mother Nature insists we use : again we drag all the way from the far south-west into Mayfair our 'black Devon rock, streaked with grey', for example. These grey streaks are 'hard' and, therefore, harmless as contrasted to the more readily available quartz or crystalline veins that look good, but dissolve quickly. You want to be careful about all this.

Rock substitutes have not been slow to come forward. For decades, now, we have been using the beautiful, just beautiful, coloured crystal lumps – streaked and veined, translucent, opaque, strong colours, delicate see-through pastels, even pure white or pitch black; easily wiped clean, impossible for algae to 'pit-into', one wipe and the horrible green stuff comes off.

Plastics, too, have played their part, as you would expect. Our 'martian' rock in gnarled, entwined, heavy threaded balls, or jutting two-tone super impositions, have long been popular. So to have artificially made plastic or fibre glass 'rocks' stamped out (hollow) in many shapes and sizes, or even as 'walls', 'stone balustrades', 'steps', 'arches', and an ever changing list of decorative items.

Fluorescent-type plastics that glow in the dark, or gleam in light are ever becoming more prominent, for rocks, for ornaments, and for sand.

Your choice is great.

There is no reason, too, why you should not use 'unconventional' things like Venetian glass vases; we drill holes in the base (sacrilege, say some) to allow a limited amount of water circulation and then use them as decorative flower pots. Often, too, we mount the vases on tall stems or columns so as to catch the light, sway in an air stream, or be positioned just in the right spot at the correct angle, which need not be vertical.

Family, or other personal motifs can be rendered non-toxic and used; as can glass, silver or even gold bangles and bracelets; futuristic strips, loops and cut-outs of chosen coloured plastics, old weathered twigs, 'logs', nicely shaped sprays cut from a tree. Have you any idea how attractive tree bark looks in strips or chunks or half-moon? If the tank is big enough why not also incorporate under-water lights inside? Waterproofing is not difficult. It is amazing what you can do with plain old bamboo sticks, cut to size and suitably arranged.

Again the choice is fabulous, and is yours. But make sure that everything is non-toxic: the glue to join bits, the screws, the lengths of wire, the elastic, the clips, springs, nuts and bolts – everything! We have all manner of ways for treating these things to render them non-toxic.

# CHAPTER SEVEN

# ARRANGING THE FURNISHINGS FOR THE HOME FIT FOR THE FISH

Having thus an almost endless choice of furnishings, which are you going to buy, and how are you going to arrange them? Unless, of course, you send for us. We go anywhere, home or abroad, to do it, and frankly simply love the creative thrill of a job well done. (Presuming you think so too!)

Your own taste, your room, and the distance away you plan to sit would have to be considered. If your tank will be alongside your chair, then detailed minuteness and finesse in colour/patterns could be appreciated, muted or gay according to taste; if sited more than six feet away then broader sweeps would increasingly tend to predominate with greater distances, the all-over glance rather so that the tank frame, its interior aquascape and the surrounding room would have a joint priority, and be taken as a whole. These are degrees of emphasis; seldom are the rules of decor rigidly hard and fast. Of course, the whole tank must always blend with you and yours.

We begin first with all the functional gadgets that simply have to be included, the heaters, thermostats, filters, lights and so on. These have all got to be kept definitely right out of sight. There must be no wires, tubes or whatever to be visible unless they are beautiful. We even make you go round and peer at the thermometer. Beauty can and will predominate, and you buy these functional essentials in combinations and sizes to fit neatly away in the far corners and reaches of your layout.

Next, the sand. An inch or two would do just the plain job of providing a base for the plants to grow in but you will need far more in order to create banks and terraces. In a rectangular 24 in. x 12 in. x 12 in. we put nearly 50 lb. weight of sand. This sounds fantastic when a quarter of that will give more than an inch of even depth.

In Chapter 8 are described the necessary but mundane details of how you wash the sand, the tools you need, and the technique of arrangement. Here, we are concerned with the artistic creative side for the moment.

Next we usually choose the rocks. These can be the very restrained natural ones only, or as is more usual mixed with the beautiful coloured crystals, for example, to be muted or gay according to taste again. The rocks do multiple work. Buried deep into the slope of piled up sand, they will hold the bank in place. We often bury practically the whole rock so that only one (very carefully chosen) side is visible and the rest is maintaining a firm grip to prevent the sand slope collapsing. Of course, the rocks are seldom used singly, but in lines, tiers, V formations, arrowheads; squat heavy ones forming a support for one or more of varying shapes : tapering fingers to reach to the ceiling (and hide the thermostate tube, say), arches, caves, terrace walls, steps winding upwards straight or zig-zag. Extraordinarily arresting is colour mixed with natural to lead up to a high-light in the distance, to have a gentle sweep abruptly terminating in one strong coloured piece, to have a circle with a colour sprinkle within, to line the winding steps with coloured walls, to have a deep cave with something strong just discernible in the gloom, to have crevices in which Angel fish can lurk, to have overhanging ledges on to which the sucking catfish can cling, to have tiny gaps and hollows into which can crawl the spiny eels. The

44

joys are endless. But firmly hidden away have been the functional heaters, etc., and firmly anchored to prevent collapse have been all sand slopes, banks and so forth. The aquascape must not only look right now, but stay so; loose gaps soon allow sand to dribble away to a flat drear waste-land. That is why you will need plenty of large rocks, buried deep, not just small pieces dumped hopefully on to the sand. They must grip, really grip, and hold their station. For the same rectangular 24 in. x 12 in. x 12 in. tank we put in rocks of a total of some 50 lb. weight. Again this sounds fantastic, again the key is that much is buried and is, therefore, functional, or is piled one on top of another, and, therefore, needs a large stable base.

Fish love, and need, little homes of their own and soon move into the crevices (flat thin fish like Angels, Scats, Discus, Gourami, etc.,) into caves (Elephant Nose fish, who are tremendous stay-at-homes), ledges, nooks and crannies. Nothing is wasted, and much is the misery of those left out if there is not enough to go round. Simultaneously there should be free open spaces where the fast, the strong, the gregarious and the gossips can throng and swirl; where fights and courtships jostle with the throbbing pulse of ever moving life. Spare too a corner, sheltered, calm and not too brightly lit, for the weak and the indisposed; where the introvert and the shy can come into their modest own. After all, you are building a home fit for the fish, and they vary in character and temperament just as much as you and I can do.

Differing depths of water are a great boon, not all fish are strong divers and swimmers – the fat and the lazy are not unknown there either, nor too are the constitutionally constructed slow movers, not to mention the floor grubbers. In their natural habitat fish tend to stay in definite layers of the water: an upturned mouth (super terminal) means a surface swimmer; a forward pointing mouth (terminal) means that mid-waters are preferred; and a downward turned mouth (sub-terminal) means that vital one inch of water right down at the very bottom of the tank must also be kept warm and clean for these. So the aquascape that provides varying depths, as well as shelters and open space, is greatly appreciated by the fish and by the humans who like the look of a beautiful arrangement. Everyone is happy! The area of air-surface governs the rate of oxygen intake into the water, not the total volume.

Plants are an essential both for the decor and for the health balance of the tank which will be discussed in Chapter 8. Plants that are delicately green and ferny, swaying near a heavy fat anchor-rock softening its hard lines; tall reed-like plants in thick jungle-clumps in which lurk the quaint-shaped Hatchet fish; neat stubby little bushes half-hiding the entrance to an arch or a cave; great big heavy leafed ones to shelter tired eyes from the light, to support the clinging sucking catfish, to lay eggs on, to have a snooze tucked up inside the curl of these fine leaves. Waving palms, spiky grass, strong tall and almost frightening, delicate dancing spheres, light greens, dark greens, red tinged, thick stems, thin stems, see-through lace work or dense thick foliage, stubby and tall – you have a choice to please the most fastidious.

To top it all, we import the plants all the year round. So even in the bleak bare depths of winter your tank can look lush and green!

# CHAPTER EIGHT

# HELPFUL HINTS ON SETTING UP THE TANK

Having got our broad picture of how we plan to furnish the home fit for the fish, we now come to the actual physical work of doing it, and the following order of sequence may help.

The interior of the tank wiped and cleaned, it is placed in position, and the 'exterior' work is tackled first. Is there a background to be stuck on to the outside of the tank at the back? Is there padding and protective hardboard, etc., to be placed between it and the window? Has enough room been left to get at the electric plugs, to fit an external filter, to house the bits of the toplight that may protrude so that it does not foul when lifted? Is the tank level, fully supported all round, in the position you want it to remain, central for example, backing up against an ornament or a picture on the wall?

Now, let us do the electric wiring while the tank is empty and dry; the toplight, which will need to be ready to switch on when we're doing the aquascape later, so that we can see exactly where the shafts of light fall; the thermostat, but make sure the heaters do not come on before the tank has been filled; the filters, especially the under-gravel ones; all the separate torpedo-switches for individually controlling the lighting, the aeration, etc., all finished, neat and tidy.

Next, the sand and rocks could be washed, this should not be done in the tank. A little sand at a time, rinsed and swirled and rinsed again and again until thoroughly, but thoroughly clean and then put straight into the tank as each portion has been cleaned, rather than be left to dribble all over the place. What did you wash the sand in? If the bucket had soap, detergent or grease in it, then all that will have gone into your 'cleaned' sand and cause trouble.

The cleaned rocks and ornaments can be laid out on clean (thick absorbent) newspaper on the floor, so that you can see them at a glance and the more easily choose the right piece when you come to dress the tank.

You may have tubular glass heaters that need to be placed horizontally flat right down in the very bottom one inch of the tank. Yet the sand is being banked up several inches high, especially at the back where the heaters usually go – right out of sight. Rather like Moses holding back the waters of the Red Sea to allow his passage through, you put the heaters flat on the floor (with perhaps half an inch covering of sand to prevent them actually heating, and cracking the tank base) and hold back the sand by building a rock wall on either side, using big squat base rocks, on which can grip the ascending ones. Over these two retaining walls you could put a cross-piece of rock or tree bark to form an arch, a longish decorative rock (or rocks) horizontally on the floor in front of the heaters and these are securely hidden and protected. Make sure the heaters do not touch the tank rear glass, or that might crack too, and for beauty's sake please thread all heater wires neatly down the tank corners, buried under the sand, until they protrude just enough to allow the glass tubes to lie flat on the sand at the chosen spot. As you probably realise the glass parts of the heaters should not be buried but they certainly can be hidden behind or even (careful!) beneath a rock.

The glass thermostat can easily hang in the corner down which you had threaded the heater wire, so hiding both

Pearl Gourami

Harlequin Fish

Kuhli Loach

Penguin Fish

Platies

from view with one tall rock, and clump of plants, or stream of air bubbles.

The filters and aerators will also have been stragetically placed out of sight, but functionally well sited. For example, if there is an inlet tube of a power filter sucking water out to be cleaned, then the end of the tube obviously should be low down right over the sand, or even in a hollow – carbon dioxide gas is breathed out by the fish and is a heavy gas tending to settle on the floor – and there should be no great impediments in the flow of the water (and dirt) across to it. Of course, the outlet tube returning the cleaned water will be in quite another part of the tank, probably placed high up.

Having hidden your heaters, say under the arch made of two retaining walls, as described, we suggest that you build your aquascape as a whole, rather than concentrate on one end of the tank at a time. Basically, the sand and rocks at the rear are piled high, you can even break water surface if you like; anchored as you go by burying deep, providing the nooks and crannies discussed in the previous chapter; and gradually tending to slope down to zero level in the front. Food dropped here then has little sand to foul.

We slope the decor not only front to back, but left to right, as well. There are no rigid rules: if good water circulation is ensured the arch for the heaters need not be central; the shallow sand where the food is given need not be in the front, although fish tend to congregate in the main feeding area; incidentally, you might have provided a subsidiary one for the weaker fish.

All the time you are doing this dressing you will be remembering, or checking, how the light from your top-light will strike. Into the areas of shade you will naturally plant cryptocorines, for example, which can manage well without too much light. Your best rocks, plants and motifs will go in the best spots, deliberately featured, with nothing distracting from them immediately near.

When the sand, equipment, and rocks have been finally arranged we normally fill the tank only partially for easier planting. The fall of the incoming water can be broken by holding a plate at sand level, or by spreading a clean sheet of paper over it, so preventing the sand being churned up and clouding the water (especially if it had not been sufficiently well washed in the first place) until the tank is about half or three-quarters full.

Plants are best grouped, single items often look thin and sparse. Opinions vary as to whether to put different kinds of plant in any one group, some people insist that this close mixing inhibits growth, but many happy combinations have survived. Most plants grow tall, too much so for the average tank, and trail their leaves along the water surface; in moderation, one or two like this can be excellent. Nearly all plants can be pruned short without disfigurement. Some like light, others not so much. As a rough guide, the thicker the stem, the more likely is the plant to protrude right out of the water. Planting sticks are a little fiddly to use at this stage but are excellent for the final touches, reaching down to straighten a tangled stem, to open or close a bunch, to lean them in a particular direction the better to harmonise, screen or sway.

Grease, oil and detergents must be totally absent from the tools and buckets you use, whether to top up, wash plants in before use, or to keep fish in. Nor, too, is it prudent to keep these things near strong smelling paints, disinfectants, soaps and so on, particularly does this apply to cloths used to wipe the tank.

When all is finished the fish tank should look gorgeous, and be balanced.

Balance is vital for fish health. Through the large air-surface oxygen is absorbed into the water, helped by the aeration and/or power filters. Varying water depths are largely irrelevant, as it is the air surface, or water circulation, that counts. This fresh oxygen is taken in by the fish who breathe it out as carbon dioxide, a harmful gas that must be eliminated. Under the action of the toplight the oxygenating plants break down the carbon dioxide into carbon and oxygen, the carbon staying to fertilise the plants themselves and the oxygen going back to the fish. This process of photosynthesis keeps the water fresh and the tank balanced. Of course, the description here given is extremely simplified and does little justice to the whole new science of water composition, content and condition as explained in *The Pelham Manual for Fish Tank Owners,* but will serve as a guide.

Any one factor will affect the whole, but you particularly need to watch : (a) excess food, fouling at the bottom and encouraging hostile bacteria, (b) excess light causing algae, (c) too many, or too big, fish consuming oxygen faster than the air-surface takes it in from the air, (d) insufficient (and more rarely, excess) plants.

When in doubt, ask your specialist dealer.

# CHAPTER NINE

# SERVICING THE TANK

Where else can you get a pet that needs so little care? That does not have to be taken out for exercise or it will mess on the carpet. That can be left without food for a fortnight while you are on holiday. That will not make a noise or annoy the neighbours while you're out. That takes up so little room, a few inches on a shelf, that lights up that part of the room into a lovely focal point, that has such beautiful colours, such intriguing shapes, such fascinating antics, that gives birth direct to live baby fish, that comes when you call, that is silent, that costs so little and gives so much.

Servicing takes only a few minutes per day, far far less than you and I demand!

*Daily Servicing*

Scarcely much more than putting on the top-light, and feeding.

If there is no filter then there is a tendency in modern cities for an oily scum to settle on the tank water surface; like a housewife skimming fat off soup you can remove this by laying a piece of newspaper flat all over the water surface, and gently drawing it off horizontally, not lifting it off vertically. As the paper is dragged off low and flat the scum is removed. Obstinate little pockets in inaccessible places like the thermostat corner, can be gently paddled out into the open with your finger, and then cleared off with paper, horizontally low and flat.

A very much more thorough way, necessary only in cases of exceptionally heavy scum, is to immerse a clean

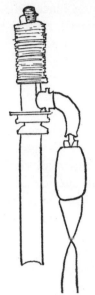

Fig. 13   Water Syphon

(no smell of pickles or tobacco!) jar tail downwards vertically into the tank. When the lip of the jar just, only just, sinks below water surface the top layer (of scum water) rushes into the jar which should be lifted gently just before it fills. Repeated operations will soon remove the top half inch of water, and all the scum.

A refinement of the above is to use a piece of paper laying flat on the surface and steered to concentrate the scum in one area into which the jar is then lowered, tail first, to suck in much scum with relatively little water.

During all these operations, the aerator is best switched off, allowing a few moments for churned up scum to rise to the surface for easier removal.

The careful aquarist will see at a glance that the water temperature is right, that the fish are not listless or having drooping fins, that there are no signs of cloudy water or of

53

fouling, e.g. sand going black where too much food has been dropped and decayed. All the work of short duration, literally of just a few minutes.

### Weekly Servicing

Using one of many available types of syphons or of underwater cleaners, the excess mulm, decaying leaves and other debris should be removed. The tank glass inside be wiped with a 'scraper' bought for the purpose, or with a clean (must be clean) small cloth and the tank topped up with new water of the same temperature as the tank (using a clean, but clean jug or bucket). We usually also wipe the sides and back of the tank glass, going 'upstream' so as not to flatten any slopes of banked-up sand.

A quick skim to remove the top scum, some food, and the whole job need have taken far less time than a man needs to shave.

### Monthly Servicing

Basically, the same as for the weekly, except that the rocks, plants and filters may want attention whether you do it, or send for us. Time required? Rather like a thorough hair wash plus bath plus pedicure.

Plants grow stalky at the bottom as they grow tall. They can be uprooted, their stems shortened down to where the foliage starts, and be replanted. New roots will soon grow.

Vallisneria, and other varieties that send out reproductive shoots, cannot be so shortened but their tall leaves and stems can be pruned from the top, or even be thinned out by hiving off parts from the main core.

The rocks can be wiped gently and slowly in situ; or be turned round to expose a new face and to bury the former one so as to allow any algae to die naturally; or be removed to be scrubbed clean (no soap, detergent or

grease on the scrubbing brush). The removal and replacement is best done one rock at a time, so as not to disturb
the aquascape too much.

The beautiful coloured crystals do not allow the algae
to grip, and a simple wipe is usually sufficient.

The filter carbon and wool may have to be changed. It
all depends on the type. A good guide is the colour of the
originally white wool; if too dark, then why not a clean
and change of both? In olden days people often forgot
the quite serious effects of fish urine and used to change
only the wool assuming that this got most of the muck,
since it was the first contact with the incoming dirty
water and had to trap all the floating debris, etc. Yet the
invisible urine also choked the activated-carbon quicker
than was often realised, so that a change of both is advised.

The filter will clean only till it is saturated. Then it
pours back water as dirty, or worse, than it receives. A
sobering thought, especially if the climate of the day is hot
and sultry.

A syphon up, not removing too much of the water, a
wipe (uphill) of the glass, a top up with water of the same
temperature, a skim, and a feed.

Imagine the work on food alone that it's taken to keep
you and me going for a month!

*A clean right-out and re-set of the aquascape*

Quite a job, with lots of bits and pieces, rather like
redecorating the kitchen, and done as infrequently.
Naturally, the professional will do it more quickly, in fact
you might even feel slightly annoyed at the way he clips
hours off the time you would have taken.

Get all the essentials ready first, so as least to disturb
the fish, and so as to be able to complete the job without
having to stop for meals.

Buy new sand, and wash, wash, wash and re-wash it

55

till it is truly clean. That is a good hour gone. Have ready at least two clean, really clean, buckets, one for topping up, the second to house the fish while you re-do the tank. Also have ready other, not necessarily clean buckets into which you can syphon out the dirty water. If the tank water is clean, though the sand is not, then additional (clean) buckets would be needed to save this clean old water for the final topping up operation.

Have ready plenty of cloths, newspapers for the floor protection. Where are you going to place on the floor the rocks, spread out in the order of removal for easier replacement. What are you going to wash them in?

Got your two nets for catching the fish? The larger one to hold in position ready to be pulled upwards, not forwards, when the fish has been driven into it by the second and smaller net. Your syphon tubes? Spare carbon and wool? Any heating unit that needs replacement? New plants?

Now have your 'tea-break' so that you are ready to do a start-to-finish-job. Oh yes, have you got something to cover the bucket that will house the fish, so as to prevent them jumping out?

Start by making a mental note of the fish that will be difficult to catch, and count their number, so that one is not forgotten. Eels, catfish, loach, small babies or neons, and other elusive ones.

Without disturbing the tank, switch off the aeration and/or filter, and the heater, though not the light, and syphon off to save in clean buckets as much of the old water as is worth re-using; perhaps half the tank.

Next remove the plants, gently rinse them in warm only water, lay them with their roots all to one end, cleaned and pruned ready for use. Keep damp.

Remove the rocks, scrub clean, and leave on floor in order for replacement.

If the filters are removable, you could do so now, and clean. If they are of the external type, outside the tank, you would probably have done so earlier.

Syphon off excess (and by now filthy water) till there are only two or three inches left. Please take great care that you do not syphon out a fish by mistake; it is very easy to do, and you may have been prudent enough to have already bought a 'fish-tail' for your syphon tube, i.e. a gadget to prevent this tragedy.

With all the plants and rocks removed, and the water down to three inches, it should not be too difficult to catch the fish, housing them in some of the clean tank water first syphoned off. You may care to plug in the heating unit into this bucket before covering to prevent a frightened or an excited fish from jumping out.

Unless the tank interior has previously been sealed with the newer adhesives that bond glass to glass, never, but never, move the tank to get rid of the messy last three inches of water. Water pressure will have normally maintained the glass bedded against the metal frame. Now that this pressure has been removed there is a distinct tendency for the glass to 'spring back' so causing a leak; moving the tank would make the tendency worse.

Instead, the water should be syphoned, the sand scooped out, the filters removed, and the tank rinsed, emptied and re-rinsed all without moving it; or without putting any pressure on the outside of the glass, e.g. by trying to wipe it clean at this stage. The inside can be wiped of course.

As soon as the interior has been cleaned, these gravel filters should be rinsed and replaced, the already-washed new sand put in, the heating unit fitted back neatly, and the cleaned rocks anchored back. All as quickly as possible, to minimise leaks.

Add new water to a depth of two inches, some ten

degrees fahrenheit warmer than normal to reheat the sand and rocks (pouring on to a clean sheet of paper spread over the sand), then all feasible amounts of the originally saved matured water, more new water warm enough to bring the whole temperature up to the usual 72°–82°F. (23°–27°C.), leaving enough room for what you plan to re-use of the water now housing the fish.

Replace plants, then the fish and top up; now the outside glass can be cleaned.

Any final touches can be done at more leisure; skim the surface, and feed the fish; then at long last, you can feed yourself and rest and admire your handiwork.

It may happen that the whole disturbance has been too much for a particularly old or particularly nervous fish. If you suspect this possibility a kindly thought would be to have a separate container for such of our weaker brethren, in which they can be housed during the cleaning. You might even make a special effort to catch them first, and to replace them in the cleaned tank, also first. For a few days afterwards you could be extra surveillant lest the fish showed signs of strain. Live foods would be appreciated.

# CHAPTER TEN

# FEEDING

The main rule has been that all the food given to the fish is eaten in two or three minutes so that no excess drops to the bottom to foul the sand. This still holds good, but progress has come to this field too.

The old crumbled bread and biscuit mixture laughingly passed off as food was soon replaced by flakes – made to scientific formulae to hold a nutritious mixture, and designed to float on the water surface long enough for all the fish to feed. There are all manner of these flakes, various colours, various ingredients, some emphasising proteins, others vitamins, carbohydrates, vegetables, etc. In large sizes for hand feeding big fish, even dyed to tinge the water to show that too many had been put in.

As change in diet is necessary for fish too, often the flakes are packed in 'menu' form, one type per day, ringing the changes over a sequence of four or seven.

A similar transformation had taken place in foods for baby fish; improving on the crumbs merely ground into finer particles came the liquidised foods, rather like toothpaste squeezed a little at a time out of a tube. Excellent for the babies, but as with their human counterparts, tending to be messy. Nurseries seldom are the tidiest place in the home. The tricky stage is when the paste foods are outgrown and solid foods are attempted. As yet there is no substitute for the finer ground particle of flake or the even more chopped up live worm. Fortunately, this transitional period is short and nearly all survive to tackle the standard sizes. It may not be long before some enterprising manufacturer enters into this 'teenage' market too!

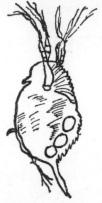

Fig. 14  Daphnia

Next came the freeze-dried revolution, as it did for humans. Processed while fresh, and then frozen, keeping its fresh quality for long periods. These come in cubes to stick on to the tank glass allowing the fish to nibble for an hour even, as the cube slowly dissolves, and ingredients cover ever wider ranges – frozen tubifex worms, mosquito larvae, ants eggs, liver, shrimp, varied formulae designed for stimulating growth, or colour, or breeding.

Now the jelly-lumps are beginning to make their mark. Put a small plastic lump in a container and leave it there permanently, so that the fish can eat when they like, for as long as they like! It really is more 'natural' as fish have very short digestive tracts and need to nibble fairly constantly for ideal health. Their stomachs or yolk sacs are ill-adapted for storing food for long periods. Mother Nature intended them constantly to be searching for foods, and, at long long last, this 'jelly type' makes it possible in the fish tank. Over-feeding, or feeding little and often are both becoming obsolete.

Vacation blocks have long been known: a sort of layer upon layer of food done in a dome shaped blob which dissolved slowly over fourteen days allowing out one small layer of food per day.

Automatic electric feeders, like a time clock that have (usually) fifteen notches to allow one per day of food for fifteen days, or three feeds per day for five days. The amount and type of food put in the fifteen 'containers' controlled by these notches being left to individual taste and choice. Excellent but expensive, their growth has been inhibited by the simple little vacation block and the permanent jelly-type foods, but they still survive.

So, too, do the truly live foods, i.e. living daphnia and live tubifex worms, for example, simply because the fish love them so, and have been known to stage hunger strikes if deprived of them for too long. In the old days we had to collect the stuff early each morning and the customer had to call each day to pick it up. Now a weekly visit will suffice because we pack the live daphnia in plastic bags pre-sealed with water, oxygen and food for the daphnia themselves so that the unit stays fresh and alive for a whole week. You simply buy seven bags, one per day, during your weekly visit.

Of course, all manner of containers are marketed to house the food in your tank : feeding rings for the floating flakes, some with trays below to catch the excess; per-forated cones or trays to allow tubifex worms to wriggle through to the tank in small numbers; gadgets for cir-culating the water past live tubifex worms so as to keep them fresh for days; containers holding live cultures of white worms, micro worms, grindal worms; and many many others.

You should have no difficulty in giving the fish a balanced varied diet. Please don't forget the vegetarians of whom there are very many among the fish, and they resent lumps of meat being thrown at them. Four or seven different tins of food, of different types and/or makes, given in sequence over the days is good. It becomes ideal, if also varied with live daphnia for instance some four times a week.

The amount you give? Sufficient for a quick meal – long drawn out banquets are unknown among fish unless the jelly-type foods start the habit. How frequently do you give? Once, or perhaps twice a day, unless you are breeding or conditioning up special specimens in which case five feeds per day are not unknown. How do you give? In various places and at various depths, simultaneously, so that the weak and slow get some too in a sheltered back-water, so that the base inhabitants like the catfish are not left out when all the food floats.

What will the fish eat? Basically anything that you and I will; no more than us do they like greasy mess, or stale stinking foods, or floating flakes trapped in an oily scrum at the water surface that should have been skimmed off first (Chapter 9). Like us, they too are adaptable. For example, if you really can't get live foods you could hang a small piece of meat, fish, shrimp, liver, prawn, roe; almost anything that does not dissolve too soon in water; cooked or raw, but washed to remove grease or blood; and hung in the tank on a bit of cotton for half an hour or so, allowing the fish to nibble. You could hang in more than one lump, at more than one depth, of more than one type. It is not too difficult to attach three lumps to one thread (bottom, middle and top), and your fish would certainly appreciate the kindness.

CHAPTER ELEVEN

# PLANT CARE

Beautiful things, necessary for the balance of the tank.

Two main kinds are available. Those that grow wild in indigenous ponds and streams of Europe and America, tending to be a little too coarse and too big for the indoor aquarium, and which can be sold (in summer) very cheaply, often in bunches. Comes winter, and these plants tend to wither and die, and the steadier advantages of buying the proper aquarium types become apparent. This second type are hot-house grown, an expensive process, are finer in texture, more suited in size and are ideal for a tank. Not everyone seems to be able to distinguish between these two quite separate groups, until they learn the hard way.

One of the troubles with the proper aquarium group was that they too, of course, grew best in summer and were then most plentiful. Yet demand for them reaches its peak in winter and its trough during the warmer months when the fish tank owner tends to go out of doors and tends to neglect his tank and his television. The problem has now been partially solved by flying over imports from Asia during the winter months. There is just one snag the discerning customer will notice. Because of 'eye-appeal' and because some people like to 'get a lot for their money' the tendency is to import bigger individual specimens of plants than is wise; An older plant is less adaptable than a younger one, and is far more likely to shed its leaves and to cut back its growth even to apparently dying (although patience will nearly always be rewarded by a new shoot). If you will consider the hot humid moist steamy air and rich river soils of Malaysia and then the sudden one-day air flight transfer to your tank, the advisability of a younger smaller plant becomes obvious; In the end it will grow bigger, quicker.

This question of rich soil has to be seen in perspective. If only the plants were to be considered then such soil would have to be provided, yet this would also encourage

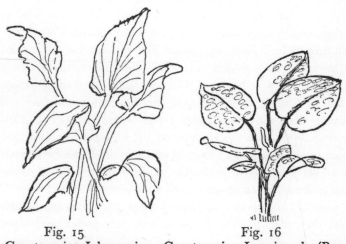

Fig. 15
Cryptocorine Johorensis
Engler

Fig. 16
Cryptocorine Longicauda (Becc.)

Fig 17
Cryptocorine Griffithii

Fig 18
Cryptocorine Lingua (Becc.)

Some Popular Plants

the growth of hostile bacteria, algae, and other things that would swing the tank balance too far away from optimum fish health. However, the dilemma has been solved in practice: at the moment of transfer of new plants, when their need for a boost is greatest, you can use one of the many chemicals specially sold to do just this job. These come either as pellets for insertion at the plant base at the time of transplanting, or more usually as liquids to be added to the tank water. Both have a limited-time action allowing the tank balance gradually to go back to normal, as the plant boost fades and the new roots thrive. You may too, increase the duration of the top-lighting by 10 per cent or so, during this sensitive period of seven to twenty-one days; of course, these are rough guides only, so much depending on local conditions. Lowering the tank temperature 2°F. can also help during this same period, particularly in the autumn when plants naturally tend to 'rest' as the sap tends to withdraw rather than rise. If, however, your new plant came from Malaysia or from the Amazon, as it probably did, with a local temperature of 80°–95°F. then a slight temperature increase would be preferable.

These suggestions are applicable mostly to the more rare and delicate varieties; many you can just simply bung in.

Certain types and sizes of fish love to uproot any plant; you could then protect it by planting in a small (decorative?) flower pot suitably holed to allow the roots to expand out into the tank base.

Plants will tell you their troubles if you will only listen: leaves that go pale, plant roots are too cramped, too hot (is there a room heater directly under the tank? Asbestos shielding would help), light too strong, or too weak; temperature too high or low; merely the normal seasonal time of rest; fish mulm or debris choking the plant; the 'crown' of the plant imbedded too deeply in the soil; not enough room for the plant to unfold; too many snails; if the base of the plant is surrounded locally by black sand, the rest being all right, then hostile nitrates are being produced instead of helpful nitrates and the tank balance is wrong; similarly if a white precipitate powder appears on the leaves

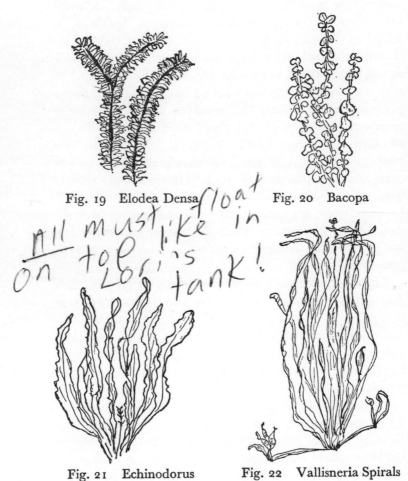

Fig. 19   Elodea Densa

Fig. 20   Bacopa

Fig. 21   Echinodorus

Fig. 22   Vallisneria Spirals

More Popular Plants

66

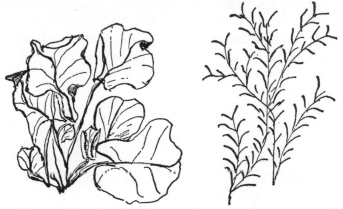

Fig. 23   Nuphar Pumilum   Fig. 24   Potanogeton Gay

in the morning but dissolves during the day, in which case the tank needs more fish, while in the former the tank needs a good clean.

Plants will also tell you their preferences if you will again listen : the lighter the green of their leaves, the more oxygen they tend to give out; a sudden darkening of the leaf colour means the plant is sulking. If the roots are relatively small and the leaves relatively big then the main nourishment comes from these and plenty of top-lighting would be appreciated but over-pruning would not. The more runners the plant sends out, the better it can stand adverse conditions like poor light (will grow in dark corners) or poor soil (will thrive in the beautiful-to-look-at clean tank base), but the more time it needs to establish itself till the runners have extended its sphere.

For plants, too, a part-change of water may help, especially if the water has gone too acid; most prefer the alkaline; chalk, or DH, i.e. water hardness is different, and softer water like rain-water might help. Just a word of caution though : the first shower of rain tends to wash all

67

manner of industrial pollutants down, so please do *not* use that.

Fertilisation of the plants by fish droppings is beneficial; but not excess urine (part change the water but maintaining the same temperature); peat is a good artificial fertiliser which most fish also love.

A whole range of quite beautiful imitation plants made of plastics is now more and more available. It excites the fury of some customers and the pleasure of others. Without doubt it is here to stay – such plants look remarkably good, never fade or fail, don't need planting and can be arranged in positions ideal for decoration, but impossible for growth.

# CHAPTER TWELVE

# BREEDING

Sooner or later you are bound to fall for this fascinating side of the hobby.

In the beginning it is very easy because of the live bearing fish, i.e. those that don't lay eggs but give birth direct to tiny but fully-formed babies, Guppies, Mollies, Swordtails and Platies to name the well known favourites. These can be so prolific that they spawn without you having ever considered the possibility, let alone having arranged ideal spawning conditions; suddenly, there they are, a shoal of tiny babies – and you're caught. You'll rush round to us, and get baby food.

And, a breeding trap. Adult fish tend to eat the fry, the rivers and lakes would be choked otherwise, and the breeding trap acts as a tank floating within your main tank in which the fry can be matured up to size. A false bottom is nearly always fitted so that the female does not eat her own fry before you can get to save them: the usual time of spawning is often at first light of daybreak. A gravid female can have anything from one or two at a time to over fifty, the usual being around ten or twenty; not unknown are several bursts of deliveries spaced hours, days or even weeks apart.

The future fry are folded head to tail inside the yolk sac of their mother causing an obvious swelling, and, as delivery time approaches, a darkening as the eyes inside become formed and prominent. The young are usually born with a supply of food tending to 'double them up'; as the food is consumed so do they straighten and begin a seemingly endless quest for food.

The gestation period varies with the time of the year, but is quickest in the main season, i.e. spring, summer, autumn; each producing one spawning. However, all manner of factors can influence the time either way – food, water consistency, depth, temperature, over-crowding, nervous disorders, etc., etc. The more nervous the fish, like the female Molly, the more uneven the period, and the more possible the miscarriage or the still-born.

For the first few weeks, all fry including those hatched from eggs, are very susceptible to almost everything, and you can be quite sure that something is wrong if the shoal grows unevenly. Did you switch to bigger foods too soon, or too late? Were there cold draughts, fry often hiding at top water under a floating leaf? Was the water surface clear of scum; was the depth too great, or even too shallow? Temperature variations, sufficient hiding places, ph and DH of water, its cleanliness ... were all these points satisfactory?

For instance, spawning under ideal conditions is often arranged in a separate thoroughly-sterilised tank of only 18 in. x 10 in. x 10 in. size with perhaps only six inches of water depth; this depth being increased by one inch per week as the fry grow. Soon they will have reached the capacity of the tank, and during the next month should be transferred to a larger 24 in. x 12 in. x 12 in., or more. Also, the original spawning water will have been scrupulously clean and of a chosen ph and DH, i.e. a chosen degree of acid or alkaline, and of hardness or softness. It may well get fouled, and when replaced should be of the same ph and DH, and should be done gradually, a little at a time, to avoid fluctuations, including those of temperature and of depth.

Young parents are clearly preferable. It sometimes appears that a female is full of roe, but has in fact merely got a middle-aged spread. It may happen too that your fish refuse to spawn for long periods; clearly, then, something is wrong, and more detailed guidance should be sought, say from *The Pelham Tropical Fish Encyclopaedia*, as the subject is too big for here. Just as an illustration, as quoted from that book, the Neons and the Cardinals needed subdued light with strong occasional shafts of penetrating brilliance and their eggs were best hatched in utter darkness maintained for five full days.

Sexing the fish, their optimum requirements for ph and DH, for temperature, foods, conditions and seasons; the period for hatching the eggs, often 24/48 hours at 75°F. (24°C.), but varying with the species; plant requirements, degree of bacteria control; foods and feeding; all such subjects are there examined. The enthusiast can really let himself go, as so very many do, because it is such fun.

# CHAPTER THIRTEEN

# WATER

Of course it's vital to the fish, and, of course, they would be very sensitive to changes in its composition and they would plead with you please to keep it fresh and clean.

As is well known fish use the mechanism sheltered behind their gill plates to extract the 'goodness' out of the water and to eliminate the noxious waste elements of their own body circulation. If this very delicate and finely adjusted mechanism is damaged, say by shock, for even an hour or two, the fish could literally 'bleed' to death – either because the membranes of the 'intake' side were paralysed and no oxygen plus beneficial salts and trace-elements were being absorbed; and because the 'retaining' side was letting out from the fish not only wastes but the beneficial trace-elements which should have been kept and without which the fish just can't live. It can die in an hour; an otherwise perfectly healthy fish, because its gill plates are temporarily paralysed by shock.

Shock is the key. In their natural habitat fish are never taken from one water and abruptly put in another, to leave one river and jump into another! They just have no protection against this form of sudden change which man imposes on them when he puts them in one tank from another, or flies them from the Amazon to London.

Given the minimum of understanding help, fish will quickly acclimatize themselves to a quite radical change, provided it is done gradually. Gradually! For example, in wild life fish are continually adapting themselves to huge seasonal water changes; when the monsoons swell the rivers and wash down vast quantities of soil, debris, vegetation and so forth, or when the dry heat of the drought shrinks the pool or the stream to relatively little water saturated in decayed vegetation. But these happen slowly.

Fluoride and chlorine are two of the worst of the fish enemies, as both will paralyse the gill plate mechanism. Fluoride has long been known deeply to affect the nerves; put in water it is regularly used to tame wild animals, to make them docile; it was so used in the wartime concentration camps to keep the inmate amenable; it is also thus used in prisons and it is the same stuff some governments are insisting on introducing into the drinking water because of some talk of saving milk teeth. The effect of fluoride on fish is markedly adverse, and you may have difficulty if it is in your tap water. Neither boiling nor filtering will remove it. We do sell tablets which temporarily modify the effects but they're not perfect.

Chlorine is far easier to elminate from the tap water. Just shaking and frothing it about would do, left in an an open-aired tank the chlorine escapes out in a few hours, or tablets are readily available capable of dissipating it in minutes.

Removal of fluoride and chlorine – both artificially introduced by man – merely puts the water back to normal, as it were, but does not make it necessarily healthy for fish. Your tank water is the fish universal provider, its supermarket; everything it needs has to come from there, and until you make changes by giving food, or by cleaning out the debris. So the fish supermarket must have a good selection of beneficial trace elements, vitamins, salts, bacteria, etc., and a minimum of hostile nitrites, for example, in the sort of stinking bog of a mess that some people laughingly pass off as an aquarium.

A whole new science of ecology has grown up as this problem of the fish supermarket has been increasingly studied. A total balance of all factors, alter any one and all the others are affected in some measure; and, of course, the question of ph and DH.

Ph measures the degree of acid or alkaline in the water; 7.0 being the neuter point, 6.0 being acid and 8.0 being alkaline. Many branded kits are sold to help you measure and alter the ph of the water, but the do-it-yourself aquarists use phosphoric acid or heavily diluted hydrochloric acid to change to more acid; and bicarbonate of soda to do the reverse. Others deliberately introduce peat or other such 'natural' products the more slowly and permanently to make the water alkaline, and there is much to be said for this.

DH, or degree of hardness, is now far more understood than it was even a few years ago, largely thanks to the German aquarists who consistently studied this aspect and have amply proved its importance. Many many kits are commercially available to help you soften the hard water of London (some 18 degrees) to a DH of only 4 or 8 that many tropical fish prefer, and in which they spawn more readily.

In earlier books and articles I have placed stress on the fact that the water need never be changed in a modern fish tank; Nor need it, but the contrast was often being made with the archaic gold-fish-in-a-bowl where the water was constantly discolouring and the fish dying because the fish was consuming the oxygen quicker than the air surface of the water was replacing it. This problem was solved in those earlier books when it was realised that a goldfish was totally unsuitable because (a) it grew too large (14 in. or more), and (b) needed so much room for swimming and consumed so much oxygen that an outdoor pond, not a bowl, was essential. People had previously been fooled just because the goldfish was so tough that it had lingered on alive in its cramped prison for a few years (or months or days!) stunted in growth and suffering in slow suffocation; in a pond it would otherwise have grown far larger and have thrived for twenty or thirty years. When the (relatively large) goldfish was replaced by the (relatively small) tropical fish, and the bowl (with a small air surface) by a tank (with a large surface) the need for constant changes of water was overcome. The tank could now be balanced, and remain healthy for years.

The new science of ecology, or study of water conditions, has taken us all a big step forward. For example, the DH, or hardness of water, just discussed one paragraph earlier. Tests began to reveal the intricate interplay of many different factors: suppose an all-over top light had not been fitted, or that there was a marked temperature difference between the tank water and the ambient air, both of which factors would tend to cause the tank water to evaporate abnormally fast; and suppose 10 per cent of the water evaporated each week, and you just topped up with new water – tests showed that in one single month you could almost triple the DH, or hardness of the water! No wonder some aquarists insisted on changing all the water at the slightest excuse. But this act of despair is easily overcome with knowledge, and a balanced healthy tank is the rule, not the exception.

However, all factors need to be considered as a whole: the top lighting, its type, intensity, duration, and angle of penetration; the plants, in their abundance and their strength; the planting medium and its bacteria forming tendencies; the number and size of the fish and the oxygen they consume and the carbon dioxide they exhale, together with their urine and their waste products. Hence the importance of the size of the tank and its cleanliness. The higher the temperature, the faster the 'rate of the cycle', and the quicker the manifestation of the result of a disturbance of the balance. And, of course, the foods you introduce, smells or toxic fumes in the air, sudden bursts of strong sunlight (millions of candle power) striking the tank, a clogged up filter that pours back dirty water, even poisoned water ... all these should be considered as a whole.

The bigger the volume of water, with healthy abundant plants, and the greater the rate of flow or circulation of the water, say through a (clean) filter, the more stable the tank balance. Cramming a quart into a pint pot usually brings problems.

# CHAPTER FOURTEEN

# TROUBLE

If fish fall sick or die there will be a cause that usually can be found and remedied; it may lie with the dealer, with you, with the fish itself, with the tank, or with the room surrounding the tank.

The dealer is assumed to be a specialist who knows his job, who keeps up with the latest medicines and who loves his fish. Such a paragon is as rare as is the perfect customer. Many a dealer is in the game just for the money; his customer is urging him to produce the goods cheaply, and both, therefore, tend to 'cut the safety factors' and so kill or weaken the fish. This is a blunt truth, becoming more so every day.

The ideal dealer will always acclimatize his imports from abroad before sale. Now this item is by far and away the most expensive of the safety factors, and the one most easily reduced – the fish 'looks fine' at the time of sale. To guarantee it longer puts up the price. Would you pay this?

Artificially bred fish now predominate over wild specimens, whether the breeding is done locally, say in Europe, or more usually in the country of origin where the climate makes (expensive) artificial heating unnecessary, and where large outdoor breeding ponds can replace small indoor tanks. But the commercial pressure to 'force-breed' is the same, i.e. to produce too many, too quickly by artificial methods of developing size at the expense of stamina. If it 'looks good' at the time of sale, and is cheap, it sells. It may also be weak, but who would pay 'the extra'? After all fish are so plentiful, so inexpensive, so easily replaced, that few of us humans spare a compassionate thought for their sufferings in force-bred conditions.

Ideally, the dealer's tanks, and your own, should be clean, never overcrowded, and big. This gives a 'poor display' with 'only a few fish in each tank', and many an undiscerning customer walks away because the dealer 'is low on stock today'. So the dealer tends to fill up, the customer tends to buy, and the poor fish tends to die. In Chapter 4 the optimum number of fish that can be kept in a tank has been discussed.

Diseases in fish has been well covered in the companion book *Pelham's Manual for Fish Tank Owners* to which reference can be made. As this ever-growing hobby of tropical fish continues to become more and more commercially important, orthodox medical science becomes further involved in it, resulting in a stream of patent medicines for fish. Most of these are excellent, as for white spot or for fungus, for example.

White spot used to be a real killer before the middle of the century. Then it got tamed by methylene blue, quinine or even sodium chloride, until the increase of atomic radiation caused mutations. The two 'normal' types of white spot mutated to five distinct strains, one of which was virtually incurable, and the disease began to be more and more widespread among the indigenous wild stocks of Asia, Africa and Latin America. In the late 1960–70 decade the position became almost desperate. Then came the spate of 'instant' cures as carefully controlled amounts of ultra-strong chemicals began to be marketed and enabled both the dealer and the customer rapidly to cure affected fish without having to remove them from the community tank. Malachite green was a typical medicine in a dosage of 1.25 drops per imperial gallon, using a 2 per cent solution made with distilled water. It did not colour the tank water, did not harm too much the plants or other fish, cured in 12–72 hours without having to raise the temperature, and needed only to have the tank water half changed at the finish.

Similarly with fungus: the new drug phenexotol being typical of the many new ones which effected rapid cures without temperature changes and without removing the sick fish from the tank. Even more important, whole outdoor ponds could now be treated because a subsequent water change, after the cure, became less imperative.

General 'cure-all' and 'preventative' medicines have naturally become fashionable; many are pure wishful thinking, some are more modest in their claims and are helpful.

A new attitude to disease is clearly emerging, as people tend to worry less and less about it, and more and more rely on patented medicines. Dealers are not slow to notice this, and fish condition at time of sale becomes more and more problematical. After all, they're cheap; and not too much attention is really paid to how the fish themselves feel.

A positive advance has been made in the understanding of ph and DH (Chapter 13) on water ecology (Chapter 13) and on filtration (Chapter 4) which will all help you in tracing reasons for the death or sickness of fish in your care.

So, too, will attention to psychological fish-needs like open spaces, lighting and hiding places (Chapter 6); changed foods and balanced diets (Chapter 10) and general tank conditions of plants (Chapter 11) and cleanliness. If your water goes green, then you know from Chapter 6 that you are giving the aquarium too much light, be it artificial, natural, or a combination of the two, and that trouble may develop if conditions get prolonged or aggravated.

So too with dirt and mulm, *including* that hidden be-

79

neath the undergravel filter even though the top sand still looks clean. Tell-tail signs like patches of black sand round the roots of the plants, like fish going discoloured, with drooping fins; listlesssness; hanging head down/up; frightened, frantic darts into unaccustomed places; hiding head-first into sand or plant thickets; accelerated breathing with or without swollen or reddened gill plates. All these are signs shrieking at you to clean the tank, or at least to part-change the water, at once. But, at once as minutes count. Please don't overlook the filter, it's almost certainly filthy and saturated.

Less violent symptoms are when fish begin to mope, to splinter off from the group and sulk, go off food, get ragged at the fins, show body blemishes; or white precipitate forms on the plants, often in the mornings; or the plants straggle, the bottom of the stems becoming bare stalks; unusual bubbles of air begin to settle or to colonise on the surface; all these are the beginning of trouble. Have you got a scum, that oily scum of Chapter 4? Are toxic fumes being sucked into your tank, by the air pump for instance? Is your proportion of plants to fish to toplighting correct? Is the fish diet too monotonous? Is there temperature stratification, i.e. layers of warm water above and cold water below (Chapter 3)? PH & DH? Too much fish urine accumulated? Anything been dropped in? Sure? Have you used cloths or tools or jam jars that smelt or had grease/detergents/polish, etc., on them? How about the temperature at 2 a.m. when the room is cold and the fire is out? When did you last clean the tank?

If the fish keeps its mouth open for unduly long periods, or has scores and swellings or abnormal markings from within which are shown on the outside (as distinct from bangs from without – in) then there is probably internal trouble, usually local to one fish. It can be food that has got stuck, or internal virus or even worms and parasites.

P. PLecostomus

Danios   Zebra

Pterophyllum Scalare

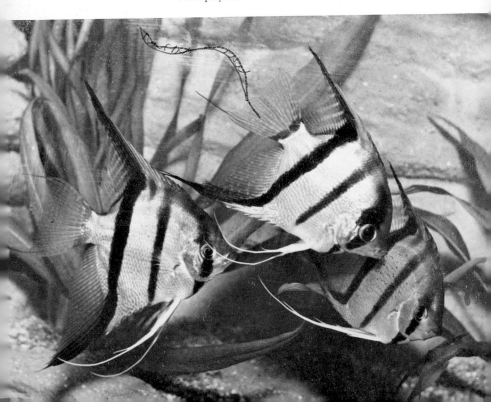

Food previously soaked in medicines, might help; so too should your specialist dealer.

Long thread-like excretia hanging from the vent is merely constipation. Some aquarists are for ever adding Epsom salts; others prefer to give more laxative foods like live daphnia, or those with strong vegetable contents. Or was the real cause of the constipation deeper and which built up gradually over a period of time finally showing through in that form (and even in some other). Was it too strong a glaring toplight, relentlessly beating down, with no possibility of shade? Lack of privacy or refuge for a weak or old fish? Loneliness? Fish like a mate, too. Or, have you been neglecting your fish tank lately, causing them to miss you, and feel unwanted!

# CHAPTER FIFTEEN
# FISH PREFERENCES

Long since passed are the days when a list of two or three hundred names would cover all that you were likely to find in a year's trading. Now it is rare for a single month to pass without a firm new addition to the range.

Gone, too, are all those neat little classifications in genus, family, orders, species and so forth. Renaming and reclassifying fish happens with a frequency and a universality that has left behind all but the most ardent enthusiast; time honoured classifications like platy and swordtail, known to generations are 'no longer valid' – to use technical terms – and have become so blurred in distinction that they are now scientifically useless.

Hence, it is now proposed merely to list in alphabetical order of popular name some typical fish, giving helpful tips on their habits and preferences, to guide the intuitive reader; if you come across a new fish, as surely you will, compare it with the better known ones, seek the points of similarity and thus find the optimum conditions. For example :

The well known Dwarf Gourami. Small, highly coloured, 'laterally compressed' body, long feelers, bright clear eyes, and small mouth pointing straight forward, i.e. 'terminal'. Had this been a brand-new fish the above clues would have given a clear index of its preferences :

(1) Small; flat clumsy body; long feelers; small mouth – obviously no good for attack and safely able to be kept with other fish.

(2) Highly coloured. A perfect camouflage in shallow waters into which pierce blinding shafts of light finding

82

their way through overhanging vegetation – so the fish is accustomed to vegetable – rich waters, i.e. soft waters of low DH say 4–8, and slightly acid of ph 6.8.

The feelers and dainty mouth denote a sensitivity and the clear eyes denote a need for clean waters. The laterally compressed body, unlike a rounded one, indicates a preference for shallowness. Hence, clean, flowing waters, crystal clear, and not too deep are an obvious choice.

(3) The terminal mouth indicating a mid-water swimmer, as distinct from a top swimmer (super terminal) or a bottom grubber (sub-terminal). Add to the clean clear waters, the bright piercing light and the overhanging vegetation, the dainty mouth and you have a mid-water swimmer used to frequent nibbling at plentiful vegetation and algae. A vegetarian fish, by preference.

(4) The defence emphasis of the body, colouring, feelers, etc., strongly suggest group unification as distinct from a lone ranger independence. The fish loves to be in shoals, and is shy to the point of being timid.

(5) Obviously a slow swimmer; therefore, a stay-at-home, The group love to form a protective colony round some (clean) crevices in the rocks, or in thickets of reed-like or bamboo-like plants.

Exposed out in the open, and alone, it would wilt.

It may here be worth repeating a short section from *The Pelham Manual for Fish Tank Owners* where this intuitive approach of understanding fish is further discussed :

'Very great guidance and hints for right care are given to you by the fish themselves if you will only look and see. The shape of the fish and the colouring give enormous clues to a loving understanding on your part, enabling you to reproduce the more easily the ideal home for your pets.'

The long, slim, torpedo body is obviously intended for

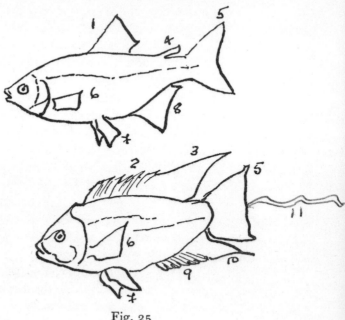

Fig. 25

| | | |
|---|---|---|
| 1 Dorsal Fin | 5 Caudal Fin | 9 Spiney Anal |
| 2 Spiney Dorsal | 6 Pectoral Fin | 10 Soft Anal |
| 3 Soft Dorsal | 7 Ventral Fin | 11 turd |
| 4 Adipose Fin | 8 Anal Fin | |

fast swimming, and will require open waters. Often this type is light coloured, silvery, streaky, sheeny, all indicating well lit waters, clear and probably fast-flowing. Such fish will love to swim against the tide of the air-pump bubbles, darting into them again and again. Zebras are a good example. All such fish need frequent and lavish feeding.

Very strong colour differentiations on a fish usually means its home waters are overgrown and that strong sunlight penetrates in sharp contrasts of light and shade. The gloriously spectacular living reds and blues of the Neon Tetra and of the Cardinal are perfect camouflage as they glide in and out of the vivid rays of light and dark alternations. The strong stripes of the Tiger Barb, or the heavy mosaic of the Gouramis, indicate similar conditions; the same with striking zig-zag or spots.

Hatchets, Scats, Discus; and the long-feelered Angels or Gouramis have a totally different-shaped body and manifestly require totally different conditions. Almost invisible to look at in front, sideways-on they have a flattened huge body, with a high back, often arching or rounded. Narrow crevices between rocks, through which they can swim in and out are ideal. Please do not have too sharp a turn or corner in the crevices so that the fish fail to navigate through. Yet too wide a channel merely defeats the purpose. Fish will love you for getting it just right. Tall slender plants like Vallisneria, in thick clumps with a gap between; or spiky plants in which they can lurk : all would be appreciated.

Most of these with long feelers venture out not too often. Fastidious about cleanliness and food, they prefer to wait for the dainty morsel rather than to guzzle. A complete exception is the Scat (short feelers) which is virtually a scavenger, going anywhere and eating anything. Most fish love to be in a shoal. These laterally compressed, high-bodied ones do so for protection, rather than the sheer joy of swirling numbers shown by the torpedo-shaped zebras. Note, too, the clean-cut vertical markings of the Angels, indicating clear waters, and contrasted with the mix-up of dots and diffused colours of the Scat – a scavenger, that goes anywhere in any water and eats (greedily) off anything.

If the breast fins (the pectorals) are strongly developed, then the fish will probably like to lurk, as just described, but make fast darts out into open clear waters, particularly if its feelers are short or are non-existent. This can apply both to the high-backed flat bodies, and to the torpedo-shaped. Obviously, too, the Hatchet and the Butterfly fish will leap, rather than dart, into the open. Being top-swimmers they frequently jump into the air, right out of the water, so that their crevices or plants must have a little of a concealed missile launcher about them.

The more arching the back, the more slow the swimmer.

The more flat, or even hollowed, the tummy, the lower down in the water does the fish tend to stay – the catfish has both the arching back and the flat tummy and it lives, as everybody knows, right at the bottom. It shows two further characteristics of bottom dwellers – a dark-coloured back and a pale-coloured tummy. An important clue. Aneus catfish are a good example. Where some others, like the Leopard cats, are lighter in colour, this simply means that its home waters are cleaner, faster-flowing and brighter-lit. You will notice that the tummy of the Leopard cat is still flat and pale, and its back still arches. Of course the upside-down catfish is just being difficult; because it lives upside-down and grubs from the underneath of over-hanging ledges, it has reversed its colouring, but its tummy is distinctly flat, even hollowed.

Eyes are a further clue. Those of the bottom-swimmers are sunken and well spaced apart, indicating the need for shade, or slightly protruding many faceted clear eyes, that seem to look in all directions at once, obviously indicating fast swimmers in open, bright, clean waters. Coupled with gay body-markings you will often find such fish to thrive best in shoals, like the Hyphessobrycon Rosaceus or the Serpae. Yet the same high colours of the body denote light and shade, so don't forget some shade, usually a little below water surface but not lower than mid-water.

Mouths are a sure index of the water-levels preferred; superterminal, or pointing upwards, for the top; terminal, or pointing forwards for mid-water; and sub-terminal, or pointing downwards, for the base-dwellers.'

# CHAPTER SIXTEEN

# SOME POPULAR FISH

In choosing these popular fish no attempt has been made to include all types. Three or four hundred would not have covered the daily commercial range!

Fish have been chosen as typical of very many others:

(a) as to type, and hence as to breeding.

(b) as to shapes, and hence as to their ideal preferences.

This book may well prove to be the first of many approaching the fish with this particular view of 'intuitive understanding', of letting the fish tell us what it likes, of our having 'eyes to see and ears to hear' so that understanding takes place.

Chapter 15 on fish shapes and preferences clearly sets the keynote.

Using this selective technique, you should have far greater success in keeping and in breeding your fish, particularly if you would care to study the fish itself, in your tank, and read the relevant section here at the same time. Quickly you will notice that no attempt whatsoever has been made to do a routine humdrum description, but rather to focus on vital 'tell-tail' points and aspects – the better to understand.

The effort of co-operation required from you is slightly more. But, then, so is the reward.

*Some Popular Fish*

ANGEL FISH, originally known as Pterophyllum Eimekei and Scalare, from the Amazon. Now found in ever increasing varieties as these firm favourites are bred all over the world. Veil-tail Angels, Lace Angels of a darker colouring, Black Angels; Lace Veil-tail. Black Veil; Marbled; White; Blue; Blushing; Glass; to name only twelve well-known types.

Lovely rounded bodies, denoting preference for deeper waters; clear bright eyes (often rimmed with a striking red) denoting love of brightly lit open spaces; striking well-defined body bands and graceful long feelers, obviously asking for clear waters and clean tanks; thin 'compressed' bodies, which love to 'make a home' in rock crevices or reed clumps and which would incline to sulk or to turn aggressive (in inverted defence) out in the unprotected open, exposed to hurly burly, and devoid of privacy.

The whole body structure suggests: (a) basic shyness, born of evolved sensitivity, that requires a mixture of a 'home' (e.g. a crevice) and open spaces into which they can sail forth, (b) in groups, like a graceful flotilla, secure in their collective numbers.

As you would expect from such advanced-in-evolution fish they require a high standard from you, the owner: clean, soft water of DH 8–12, neutral ph, rich in trace elements. This is the main key. If your local water 'suits' them, they will breed readily.

Fastidious, of course, they will wilt or go on hunger strikes, get ragged fins, mope in corners, if you are failing in providing right waters. They require good and, especially, varied foods; live foods particularly welcomed; and personal attention from you. The degree to which they can respond to the human voice is flattering.

Temperature tolerance is wide, 72°–75°F. is excellent. They grow to 6 in. or more, and have those lovely extended dorsal and anal fins that impart such grace and dignity.

Courtship is of the normal chiclid type with rather violent trials of strength through locked jaws and somewhat rough play. Once mated they tend to stay in faithful pairs, and to take great care of the young. Typical of their shy/aggressive duality they have been known to eat their eggs or even their fry 'in order to protect them' if their breeding privacy is disturbed.

Dim lighting, clear-flowing aeration, a minimum of chemicals, and the eggs hatch in 48 hours at 76°–80°F., growing rapidly in the usual way. Please don't overdo ozonisation.

Two female Angels have been known to pair off and to produce infertile eggs; sexing is not always easy and self-chosen pairs are obviously best. The males have the following characteristics: anal fin sharply angled from the body; pointed genital papilla, angled backwards; protruding lower jaw; slightly more circular body but a bright light shone sideways through the fish shows a flat topped intestine with a depression in it. For the females the following clues will differentiate: straight anal, well developed; rounded genital papilla; examination sideways through a bright light shows a circular intestine, including the top. Distance between ventral and anal fins is relatively great and is straight lined. Viewed head-on the female body is more full behind and below the pectorals.

APHYOSEMION AUSTRALE. Typical of the beautiful 'tooth carps' from West Africa, in gorgeous colours and a 'torpedo-body with appendages'. There is a strangeness, an ultra-colouring, an intensity of feeding and living, a clear impression of being 'forced and pushed' that gives the clue to its home surroundings and, therefore, of its unusual preferences.

It comes in fact from shallow pools and rivulets that form in the tropical rainy season, flourish for a few short hectic weeks, and then dry out. No wonder its colours are intense, as though heightened by fear (of inevitable drought), depicting preference for strong overhead lighting shaded in patches. The fins grow so luxuriously that the waters would have to be shallow and protected. Hence small tanks, only 4 in.–9 in. deep are an obvious choice.

Their very definite mouths, super terminal or terminal according to species, denote an intensity in search for food, so that frequent feeding is called for.

At once it will wilt in dirt or in hard water. When the rains come the eggs left buried from the previous year hatch almost at once, while the water is still clean, bacteria free, soft, and acid; and the temperature has not yet risen to dry out the pools. Hence, DH 8, ph 6.8, $74°–76°F$., and ozonisation will help; so, too, will a peat base.

It appears that the eggs cannot hatch by themselves as the outer covering is extra thick to protect them during the long drought. The rains soften the 'peaty' dried vegetation of the previous year, develops the growth of beneficial bacteria, which eat the outer-shell of the eggs, allowing them to hatch. The fry then eat the bacteria and hasten on to mature quickly, mate and spawn before the pool dries out, imprisoning next year's eggs in the mud.

Hence the intensity with which these tooth carps live : can you blame the males for staking out a claim and for fighting off potential rivals, i.e. other males of their own kind. They do not seem to be too interested in others – after all their total life span is only months.

Hatching period for the eggs is dependent on the local circumstances of the pool or rivulet, and hence varies from two to fourteen weeks! The eggs seem easily to get 'frightened', to 'reverse gestation' and to prepare to hold out through a drought till next year. Then, if they 'get their confidence back', they restart gestation and hatch, weeks late. Exactly what causes this 'fright' is difficult to say, but shrinking water depth and increased temperature as the drought approaches are two obvious possibilities.

Equally obvious is a decreasing cleanliness of water as debris blows into the newly formed pools and subsequent alteration of ecological factors, notably DH and PH. So an even temperature, clean soft water, constant depth, unaltered lighting, ph, DH, frequent feeding, positively no draughts in the shallow tank (whoever heard of a cold draught of air in African summers?), shady plants, dark peaty base and your Aphyosemion Australe will thrive and live and play and jump (watch out!) with an intensity you will not forget. That and their beautiful colours make them great favourites.

There are many kinds, of course, blurring one into the other, but still known by their old fashioned names like Aphyosemion Calliurum calliurum, calliurum ahli, calliurum schmidti and a whole group of 'non peaceful' ones like schontedeni, gardneri, or elegans. Basically there are the mid-water types and the bottom four-inches-of-water types. An obvious clue is the mouth – super terminal (above), terminal (middle) and sub terminal (bottom). The more 'definite' the mouth and the fewer the trailing-flowing fins, the more you need to watch out for attacks on other fish – aphyosemions like eating, fast!

APISTOGRAMMA RAMIREZI. Typical of the 'dwarf chiclids' from Venezuela, and a firm favourite.

Its strong colours, stubby body and snout, relatively big finnage all denote its general peacefulness, though the purposeful-appearance of strength indicates that it will stand up for its rights. Particularly when defending its home, the body is obviously not that of a fast, far swimmer, and it is in fact a great home-lover. Give it its own cave, hole or hollow and it will live and let live, merely shooting off intruders.

True to its good colouring it likes strong overhead light penetrating through leafy foliage; clear eyes, denoting clean water; somewhat compressed body denoting shallow depths.

Slightly alkaline ph 7.0 to 7.2, DH 8–10, 74°–76°F. and water depth of 10 in.–12 in. soon grow it up to its matured 3½ in. length. Has a marked preference for cleanliness, green-stuffs, and sand terraces interspersed with rocks, flower pots, caves, arches and so forth.

Not always easily to sex, the female usually has stronger red on her flanks in breeding condition and shows a short genital papilla. But she often takes the spawning initiative and can look very like the male.

Spawning can be induced by a 2°F. temperature increase, and the adhesive eggs are usually well hidden on previously cleaned rocks or even leaves. 48 hours at 78°F. is usual for hatching and the fry are able to take infusoria, brine shrimps and micro worms in quite rapid progression, reaching the stage of eating small daphnia in two weeks. Both parents guard the brood, with the female tending to be the dominating partner.

APISTOGRAMMA AGASSIZI is also famous, with similar characteristics : slightly accentuated, e.g. its finnage is not quite so pronounced, so it is not quite so peaceful. The female is even more bossy than for the ramirezi and definitely hen-pecks. Her breeding colour on the flanks is yellow with black spots but even takes on the male colouring in the fins (blue-green with luminous shiny dots) when being particularly assertive. During care of the brood she frequently banishes the male to the outer regions, allowing him to come home only when it suits her.

The eggs may take four days to hatch at 78°F. and often number two hundred.

Both species are fastidious as to conditions, witness their definite body colourations and clear eyes, and are liable to sickness if things are not right. So, too, of course, with

the eggs and the fry. Medicines should be used in homoeo-
pathic doses rather than in the more orthodox allopathic,
i.e. in very small doses.

BARBS (many of the Puntius genus). There are literally
dozens upon dozens of different trends of these lively,
playful, almost boisterous, fish, and, as an example, let
us take the *Tiger Barb*, scientifically known as Tetrazona.

Its clear cut markings, golden sheened body, slightly
arched, all suggest clear waters, warm temperatures, nimble
movements rather than long swims, bright light, and some
definite plant shading. Hidden barbels denote keen interest
in food, and lack of pugnacity denote a preference for
shoals.

Liable to hang head (or tail) up if the water is not
clean enough, i.e. has too much invisible fish urine or
hostile bacteria in it, otherwise they can stand almost anything, anybody, or any food. Often accused of being fin
nippers, they tend to play among themselves and to leave
others alone provided there is a shoal of at least three or
four, and providing hiding places are available as well as
open waters.

Being boisterous by nature, so too is their mating which
conforms to the normal pattern except that the eggs tend to
get scattered in the frenzy. Otherwise the deails are much
as described for the Rasbora, although the Barbs are not
as fussy over the water. DH 8–12, ph 7.0, 77°–79°F., and
well-oxygenated tanks suit them very well.

The older the fish, the more the body arching becomes
pronounced; in case of general listlessness, a change of
water and a lowering of DH from 8–12 to 4–6 is almost
certain to help. Usual length 2 in.

ROSY BARB. (Barbus Conchonius) was one of the original
imports, and is still in demand, though its larger size of
$3\frac{1}{2}$ in. and its relatively drab colours have lessened this.

The high colouring 'rosy' of its name happens only in breeding condition.

Its drab 'sluggish' colours indicate its capacity to stand lower temperatures (down to 60°F.), and is tough enough to survive adverse treatment.

GOLDEN SCHUBERTI BARB is a descriptive name that still sticks although scientifically it is 'no longer valid', having been merged with Barbus Semifasciolatus, amongst others.

Its relatively quiet colouring indicates its indifference to temperature, and it will breed at only 72°–74°F. or less. Undemanding, it is easily spawned and reared and hence is still a favourite. Length 4 in., peaceful, unobtrusive, and adaptable.

Our three examples have focused on the boisterous and the quiet, the colourful and the plain, the large and the small. In a genus where there are hundreds of types, such variety is to be expected.

BETTA SPLENDENS (Siamese Fighting Fish). One of the most famous of them all. By now most people realise that these can safely be kept in a community tank, although not with another male of their own species, and, also, not usually with a female lest they start protecting (or hating!) her and causing trouble all round.

Magnificent finnage; ever improving with new strains, some transparent, some coloured, some shot and flecked. In gorgeous colour sheens; pure or mixed, with red, blue, green and albino predominating; but by no means being exhaustive. Growing to a sturdy 3 in., these dominating males are short-lived, thirty months or less, and ride rough-shod over their terrified females who are shorter finned, paler, smaller, and no match whatsoever for their vigorous partners.

The long torpedo body indicates swift movement, but is

too encumbered with (beautiful) finnage to allow for long swims, and the fish is a real stay-at-home; in fact, this can only too readily develop into sulks in corners if conditions don't suit it. The flaring gill plates and imposingly extending fins preclude gregariousness, with others of its type, but a lofty disdain of lesser breeds. High colouring points to its preference for warmer, clean, waters of 77°–84°F. The business-like mouth will tackle most foods, but would scorn the unworthy. Algae is also taken willingly as its superb colouring surely indicates bright waters heavy with growing plants. Obviously, it is a lurker rather than a wanderer, and needs a 'home' of its own.

Having an auxiliary breathing apparatus, it periodically surfaces to gulp air, and is therefore very tolerant of water conditions. This labyrinth breathing makes understandable its breeding characteristics: a floating nest of air bubbles, coated with saliva and anchored where surface plants and algae abound, is used to house the eggs. Constantly the burst bubbles are more than replaced, usually by the male alone, and any fallen eggs replaced in the nest whose increasing thickness lifts the eggs more and more until they are clearly visible from the top. They are very sensitive indeed at this stage to cold draughts or to dust and to oily scum.

When hatched the fry hang vertically from the nest, wriggling back to position if dislodged, but start swimming vertically after a few days if infusoria food has been plentiful. Up till now, the male is usually very protective of the brood, but directly this begins to break up and they swim independently he should be removed.

Water level can be kept down to 4–6 in. during breeding, being gradually increased the usual 1 in. per week. Sunlight, periodic water changes to help remove some of the over abundant foods usually demanded; and, to repeat, no draughts, oil or dust, will help ensure good results. Water can be DH 4–6, ph 6.8–7.0, seasoned with peat, and kept at 78°–82°F.

Males are very fussy about the females they accept, and their courtship is rough in the extreme. It is essential to condition up the female separately, introduce her gradually to the male, say for an hour at a time separated off in a jar or by a partition, before putting them together in the prepared tank during late evening. The female may need protection if she does not please or is not in sufficiently full spawning form; otherwise mating could easily start in the early morning. The exhausted female should be removed as soon as it is over.

Grown fry of almost three months can still be kept together because sex differentiations and finnage have not yet developed. At a body length of one inch the male anal fin begins to incline obliquely downward; staying parallel to the body in the female. Separation time is rapidly approaching.

BLACK WIDOW (Gymnocorymbus ternetzi) Paraguay. $2\frac{1}{2}$ in. A good old oldie that every aquarist seems to have kept since the early part of this century. Its clear, neatly defined, contrasting black markings on a silver green sheened body, its bright, red rimmed eyes, all show its need for clear waters, well lit, with strongly growing foliage interspersed with open spaces. A firm super terminal mouth shows its self-confidence, its ability to look after itself, yet not aggressive enough to be pugnacious; the fish gets on well with others, and is also happy in a shoal.

Its laterally compressed body, fairly rounded, indicates a mid-water fastish swimmer, tending to go to top waters in search of food since the mouth is super terminal. A certain restlessness and mobility that lessen the need for a 'home'.

Males have the usual characteristic of Characins, i.e.

Scatophagus Argus

Barbus Schuberti (These are fun to find dried up in your bed.)

Chilodus Punctatus

a hooked anal fin. Also as usual the more humped the body, the older the fish. Fading colours also indicate old age, although these can be brought on, of course, by adverse conditions or by fright.

Easy to keep and spawn, the eggs are free-scattered and hatch in 48 hours, they are adaptable but will thrive at DH 6–8, ph 6.8, 78°–80°F. They love dancing aeration and will dive and play in the bubbles. To rest they often hang motionless under a shady leaf, going pale as they sleep. Sensitive to foul waters they protest by going off balance and hanging head down, patiently waiting for you to part change the water. They will eat almost any reasonable foods, preferring flesh to vegetables.

New varieties now have truly magnificent veil tailing fins, which are strikingly graceful and taut, and yet maintaining their strong black colouring.

CARDINALS. (Cheirodon Axelrodi) Length $2\frac{3}{4}$ in. Rio Negro. Breathtaking in its beauty, with the 'living colours shining from within – out'; a wide luminous red band the full length from the mouth through the eye, to the caudal peduncle; bordered below with a phosphorescent red band from the gills to the tail. It has displaced the world renowned Neon tetra for beauty, and is slightly larger as well; although the two are similar.

Their intense 'living' colours are perfect camouflage in shallow heavily overgrown waters, pierced by blinding shafts of strong sunlight, and give strong hints to their home requirements. Clean, clear, soft waters; flowing over and through heavy vegetation, hence acid; warm; and not too deep, open spaces bordered by sheltering thickets.

Cardinals come in fact from the overhung rivulets of the head waters of the mighty Rio Negro where the emerging waters are clean, pure and 'bacteria-free', i.e.

DH 2–4, ph 6.5–6.8, peat covered base, dark in colour, 75°–82°F., depth 12 in. or so.

The male is slimmer, less rounded, and his green line is more straight. A strong light shone sideways shows a swim bladder tapering towards the tail, leaving a free space between the bladder and the viscera. The female bladder is rounded and the free space is filled by the ovary. Young adults are obviously best for breeding and should be allowed to pair off naturally, being conditioned up till their colours are intense, using, for example, chopped up white worms, brine shrimp eggs, tubifex and daphnia. September/October and April/May are good breeding times.

Absolute cleanliness is the rule. The 18 in. x 10 in. x 10 in. breeding tank with spawning nylon mops or soft plants, absolutely should have been sterilised; filled to 6 in. or so with water as already described, leaving plenty of free swimming space round the mops or plants; and, last but by no means least, allowing strong exterior-to-the tank side lighting (not overhead) to filter through translucent green paper.

As is usual the separately conditioned female is introduced first, and the male at dusk. Sometimes spawning follows automatically next morning, sometimes not. In which case, alter the temperature 2°F., the water depth an inch, reposition/reduce/increase the mops, recheck for cleanliness; is the base covering of peat enough; did you use previously-soaked-in-peat water; try aeration; is the light too dim/strong or not diffused/streaky enough? One or more of these factors is almost certain to work.

Rapid darts into the thickets start the spawning, which get more frenzied, side by side, quivering and touching – and scattering the semi-adhesive eggs. Those lost at the bottom are more likely to be attacked by bacteria than the ones protected by the steriled mops or plants. Three hours is usually enough, and the parents can be removed.

Fear of bacteria is the next main hurdle, and complete and total darkness should now envelope the tank for five full days. a mild disinfectant of methylene blue or of acriflavine may help, so, too, does very gentle aeration, and a temperature of 75°–78°F.

During the darkness the eggs should hatch in forty-eight hours, live off their yolk sacs, and be free swimming (and starvingly hungry!) when the light is progressively restored after five days. Frequent feeding on newly hatched brine shrimps, and growth is rapid.

The fear of bacteria, heightened by the frequent feeding, causes some breeders to transfer the growing fry to new tanks (of identical waters) rather than merely part change the waters. Of course, the water depth is increased an inch a week, up to say 12 in.

The *Neon Tetra* (Hyphessobrycon innesi) are similar, and slightly smaller. They come from more or less the same types of rivulets as the Cardinals, and can be kept and bred as just described.

Both are hardy, peaceful, and beautiful; looking best in shoals of six or more, viewed by side lighting obliquely across a dark base.

The golden *Glow Light* Tetra (hyphessobrycon gracilis) also qualifies with its intense gold stripe, shining from within-out, and has almost identical requirements. Except that it is slightly less fastidious, and can stand another two or three degrees of temperature, tending to feel the cold more than the other two.

Discus Symphysodon (original red), Symphysodon aequifasciata haraldi (Blue Discus), Symphysodon aequifasciata axelrodi (normal brown discus), Symphysodon aequifasciata aequifasciata (the green discus) to mention but a few of the names of but a few of the types of this new *Queen of the Aquarium*, positively the favourite of favourites. Scarcely known before 1957!

Its shape gives a clear index of its ideal requirements : beautiful circular body, laterally compressed, and free of distortions – deep tanks essential; rock crevices, reed hide-outs, a nice home of its own, obviously a must; perfect symmetry, hence highly evolved, hence expects a high standard from you, and just anything will not do! Short feelers, often coloured; fastidious, to be sure, proper foods must be properly served. Clear, red-rimmed eyes and mosaic of high colours : clean, well lit waters, lavishly sheltered by plants and rocks, flowering through and over lush vegetation with strong lights beating through in alternating light/shade patterns; warm. Defensive, rather than aggressive : hence shy, a stay-at-home, gregarious; pine when alone and neglected, flourish in a shoal, and respond readily to your love and affection. Will know your voice; will miss you and mope when you are absent. Tameable and lovable. A true 'queen of the fish tank', requiring regal, roomy quarters. Not to be cramped into a bed-sitter! DH 2–4, ph 6.8, 76°–84°F., clean; filtered.

Yet Discus are adaptable, increasingly so as many strains are being widely bred in captivity; the colours shade, merge and alter according to local conditions and moods. A light base, mulm, poor lighting, insufficient shade/light contrast, lack of hide-outs, overcrowding and exposure to noisy/flickering/banging/hurly burly soon affects their nerves. Much more so than poor foods or hard waters.

Mild medicine like Aureomycin ($\frac{1}{4}$ gram per gallon) can help, so too, can the companionship of the gentle Dwarf Gourami; change of water, rise of temperature, and hand feeding with chopped white worms but done in the immediate vicinity of their home, are well-known stand-bys for difficult periods and moods. A new 'house' built of matured tree-bark; tall, but roofed-in, not too wide apart, but with fairly hidden entrance and a separate exit, is also likely to please. So too will peat.

The male anal fin is more pointed at the end towards the tail, his genital papilla tends also to be pointed, and the ventral fins hang down and then curve backwards in a crescent shape. More bull-headed, his colours are deeper particularly on the head area, and just behind, and in the fins; he is larger in total size. The female genital papilla is cone shaped and rounded off; her ventral fins sweep straight down, curve, and sweep again, to form an S shape, her body bands are slightly less clear-cut, and yellow often predominates over red in her colours but not after spawning takes place when the male, too, seems then to emphasise the yellow.

Separately conditioned parents, can be introduced to the tank which is brightly lit and well planted as already described. A lowering of the light intensity, and a 2°F. raise of temperature often induces the relatively mild love play, and some 200 adhesive eggs are carefully laid on the cleaned and prepared surface. Often they are laid in neat rows, from above down, and fertilized at the same time. Hatching in forty-eight hours the fry hang on for another two days before becoming free-swimming; laggards are often sucked clear by the solicitous parents.

As you would expect, privacy and freedom from noise, light flashes, or other distractions are essential. Frightened parents have been known to eat their eggs or fry.

Given reasonable conditions the parents are constantly fanning, cleaning, shepherding the unruly brood, and, especially at nightfall when the fry seem to delight in refusing to be adhered to the chosen shelter.

The parents allow the fry to suckle an excretion, or sort of mucus, covering the whole body; one parent in turn acts as 'host' allowing the brood to nibble all over his or her body. At change-over time the relief parent swims alongside, enticing the brood, while the other suddenly darts off. The fry suckle this mucus for very many days, and a 'foster parent' usually a second female, has been introduced to help things along, strange as this may seem. Once the fry are truly free swimming and are eating well, it is relatively rare for them to be attacked by their parents, including 'foster' ones. Newly hatched brine, shrimps, grindal worms, tubifex 'pre-chewed' by the parents, and sifted live daphnia are all taken.

Once the fry grow to one inch or so, usually in a week, the parents should be removed. Relatively frequent part-changes of water, help develop the disc shape in about twelve weeks; sexual maturity takes another twenty months.

DWARF GOURAMI (Colisa lalia) India. Length $2\frac{1}{4}$ in. In Chapter 15 the ideal preferences of this delightful and truly beautiful fish have already been detailed. So too have its breeding habits, which are standard for the labyrinth breathers or anabantids, as described for the Betta Splendens, except that the male is not brutal.

Very sensitive to water depth, an alteration of even one inch can affect it, the cleanliness of water, and to draught-free warmth.

The male dorsal fin is definitely larger, more pointed and, of course more colourful as is his whole body.

DH 4–6, ph 6.8–7.0, 76°–84°F; aeration and heavily planted tanks, cleaned and well lit. Respond favourably to Acriflavine.

Other similar favourites are the Lace Gourami, or Pearl Gourami (Trichogaster Leeri), growing to a gorgeous five inches, but always staying peaceful. Less striking are the Thick Lipped Gourami (Colisa Labiosa), growing up to four inches, and of course, the variations; the Honey, the Croaking, the Kissing, the Chocolate, the Marmarota, the

Opaline and the Jewel Gouramis to name seven of the more popular. Beware of 'Three-spot' or Blue Gourami which definitely can be pugnacious.

All these fish eat Hydra, and will soon clear an affected tank if given no other foods.

ELEPHANT NOSE. Mormyrids. Upper Nile. 5 in. A quaint lovable fish that has got itself a bad name, mostly undeserved. Basically it is ultra-shy, ultra-frightened and, therefore, 'appears aggressive' in exaggerated self-defence. Just give it a home of its own where it can feel safe and secure, and it will watch the world go by, staying peacefully in its immediate area and bothering no one. In fact, it won't even leave the home area for food, and will starve if not fed there. This applies to each Elephant Nose you keep; two specimens will need two, preferably three quite separate hide-outs; the third 'spare' one helps each to feel more secure in the one its got. Even spawning pairs demand this, before and after the acts.

The whole appearance of the fish bears out the above remarks – obviously no good for attack, clumsy body, tiny mouth at the end of its elephant-like trunk; its sole real defence is to be able to emit a mild electric shock, too weak to harm but just enough to afford some protection.

Thickly embedded eyes and drab colouring clearly mark it out to be a bottom grubber, in mud, silt, decaying vegetation, mulm, etc; and obviously in dim light. Hopelessly inadequate to cope with fast-flowing movement in open bright areas they will hide all day in such conditions and come out only at night, dusk and dawn. Yet given a soft, dark coloured bottomed tank, set up as indicated, full of nooks and crannies of old flower pots, caves, arches and tree bark; lit with diffused, slightly murky light; and they will play all day long in and round the home, tossing a leaf like a beach ball. Once tamed to the sound of your voice they will hang on your every word, and positively will wilt if you then neglect them – their security will have been shattered.

As you would expect from the dainty mouth the fish are personally clean, and will keep their home thus; nor too, will they eat any old foods. Most clean small morsels are acceptable, usually picked up 'from above' off the ground; they do not seem to like to have to 'reach up' for it, and, of course, won't leave the home area. Food particles are sucked in, rather than chewed (although there are a few teeth) and need to be appropriate in size and texture.

DH 4–10, ph 6.2–7.0, 76°–80°F.

Many varieties exist, with long and short trunks, and some with really pleasant markings. Sizes vary too.

HARLEQUIN. (Rasbora Heteromorpha). Length $1\frac{3}{4}$ in. Typical of many of its genus that come from the Malayan archipelego. Included here partly because it's a good old favourite, beautiful and hardy, and partly because of the ever growing fashion of keeping only small-growing fish; genuinely tiny jewels; in small, separate tanks, neatly matched in patterns, tiers, or rows.

The body markings are not a mosaic of various colours, but clearly are grouped in one definite triangle on relatively a plain background; the background being clean and reflective; all of which suggests a love of brightly lit open spaces (look at its featured red-rimmed eyes), clean, clear waters, not particularly overgrown or shaded. Its body is medium-slim, tending to a balanced top plus below arching, indicating a medium swimmer, and, lacking offensive characteristics, tending to be gregarious and preferring to be in shoals. So it needs open swimming space, but not too much or too violent, i.e. not a strong current for instance, a backwater rather than mid-stream. Medium depth of water is also suggested.

In fact, the fish comes from clean, gently flowing shallow creeks carpeted by sand-cum-fallen vegetation. The waters are extremely soft, right down to DH 2, and this is one main factor for its health and for breeding.

It likes high temperatures as may be guessed from its body sheening, well-formed scales, and nimble movements; nothing sluggish or cold about a Rasbora.

Eating most foods readily – it lacks the fastidiousness of long feelers, or the greed of short barbels – it can be conditioned up for spawning, using DH 2–4, ph 5.5 to 6.0, 75°F., clean sandy base covered with some peat or cryptocorine leaves, the spawning act can be induced by raising the temperature 3°–5°F., in a thoroughly sterilised tank.

The male colourings are greater, including the red of the eye, and the lower tip of the triangular wedge is slightly forward reaching. It is slimmer than the female, whose plumpness round the base of the triangle shows especially from above, and causes a slight blurring of the markings. The gold colour seems to predominate in the female, rather than the red of the male.

The spawning act itself is normal, the pair staying quietly in mid water or under a protective ledge or leaf until one (usually the female) takes the initiative to start the frenzied spawning chase enticing the partner over the chosen thicket. Then, motionless quivering, upside down, brushing the chosen thicket or leaf with the vent, the male clasps the female wrapping his tail round her, to squeeze out a dozen or so adhesive eggs at each embrace; repeating the chase and embrace until nearly two hundred eggs can have been extruded and the female is exhausted.

The parents removed, great care now has to be taken to protect the eggs from disease, although the tank had previously been sterilised. Many breeders keep the tank in darkness for five days; some add mild chemicals like methylene blue. Hatching in 24–36 hours, the fry are free swimming in another five days. The water depth can now be increased an inch per week, and the DH gradually brought up to a more normal 8–10. In passing it could be noted that the extreme softness of DH 2 suggested above is for wild specimens straight from Malaysia. Tank bred specimens abound, and these have been kept and bred in all kinds of water.

Other firm Rasbora favourites are Maculata or Uropthalmus for the smaller ones and many larger varieties like trilineata, einthoveni, pauciperforata, etc. Naturally these distinctions are less clear cut than they used to be, and new types are regularly coming forth.

HEADSTANDERS. Chilodus Punctatus. Guyana. 3 in. Typical of the fish that do not float on an even keel, these stay head down.

The pronounced arch of the back, the small terminal mouth (which has small teeth behind the lips), the general slow-moving carriage, and the slightly 'piercing' eyes give a clue to its preferences. Not too much open space with attendant rough and tumble; hence a 'live and let live' type. A nibbler, it might even have degenerated into a scavenger but for the dainty mouth, constantly requiring to peck at food, its drab colours suggest drab not-too-clean places – tangled, overgrown thickets round fallen branches and twigs suit it fine. Soft sand, even silted mud, decaying vegetation; all these help it, so too does a humid, oppressive sort of swampy warmth, and cold draughts would certainly not be welcome any more than would be swift water flow. It loves algae, and hiding places.

DH 6, ph 6.6, 78°–86°F., are suggested although its tolerance is wide, provided the temperature is kept high.

Of course, there are many variations on this old standing

favourite, that tolerates dirty water, even accentuating its rather drab colours therein.

Relatively easy to spawn, it helps to have the top lighting raised well above water surface and focused to alternate between strong penetration and diffused straggle. Some 150 eggs hatch in three days at 80°–84°F. and are free swimming in a week; an increase to 86°–88°F. helps. The parents are not particularly solicitous and should be removed after spawning. Draughts are fatal, as already stressed.

KHULI EELS. (Acantopthalmus kuhlü). Length $3\frac{1}{2}$ in. Typical of the ever-increasing number of eels now imported, with varying markings, thickness and lengths. Peaceful and industrious, they are largely dark or dusk (i.e. half light) enthuasiasts, and tend to hide away in bright lights. They entwine round plants, jam in between rocks, literally burrow into the sand, yet can swim at a fantastic speed if disturbed. This is what really keeps them from being even more popular: they are so fast that dealers hate having to catch them, at the cost of a wrecked tank decor.

Obviously they like burrowing and rummaging among decayed vegetation, mulm, twigs, reed-like plants, thick-stemmed sturdy ones, old flower pots, rock caves, and so on. A bare tank is hopeless for them. The eyes are covered by a transparent skin, for protection, as they wriggle through the most unlikely places and indicates that they like clean waters, this is important. Gregarious in the extreme, you often find a clustered colony of them hidden in the tiniest of hide-outs. Eat anything that fits their small mouths. When unhappy or frightened they swim restlessly up and down. Given a big enough tank they would move right away from an unpleasant area, yet they are firm home lovers once they have found a nitch that suits.

For spawning they leave the accustomed bottom part of the tank, and whirl and frenzy, right at top water, which then must have many branched twigs and, preferably, shady leafed surface clumps for them to love – nuzzle and entwine in. This much we might have guessed from their adaptable, swift, easy of movement and freedom from fixed restrictions. The waters should be clean, soft slightly acid, aerated strongly, and warm; DH 4–8, ph 6.8, 75°–82°F. Muted streaky lighting helps.

PENGUINS. Thayeri obliqua. Amazon. $3\frac{1}{4}$ in. As usual, an intuitive look at the fish soon gives an idea of its preferences.

Clean silver-golden sheened body, bright eyes; obviously likes open, clean, well lit waters; particularly in view of the neatly drawn unsmudged, black line transversing the whole length from the eyes to the far tip of the tail.

Yet the appearance is certainly not one of attack; it even lacks a little in confidence. This is accentuated by the peculiar way it always hangs tail-down, when at rest, heightened by the extra long lower fin of the twin-finned tail, with the black line curving down to the furthest and lowest corner. Obviously then it needs the support of a shoal, and will tend to hide among plants if alone.

The slightly super terminal mouth is business-like and the body suggests a fair turn of speed so that undue liberties should not be taken with this fish. Especially the one that has been kept alone, hiding in plants, and getting fretful – such a one has been known to take it out of a weaker fish that approached too near. The mouth, too, also indicates that it prefers to reach up for its food, and would not be too happy at having to leave top-waters to go down to the bottom for sunken particles.

A great favourite; easily kept and spawned. DH 2–4, ph 7.0, 75°–82°F., aeration, and clean bright waters, frequently changed, suit it well; as do tall, well grown plants.

PIPE FISH. (Syngnathus spicifer). Ceylon. 7 in. Quite distinct from the African varieties which tend to be longer, and which often need salt or brackish water. These relative newcomers from Ceylon also like brackish water but adapt to fresh fairly easily.

Care has to be taken over the food, which has to be taken to the fish, rather than the other way round. Like the Elephant Nose, it too has a small mouth more given to suck than to chew; located as a small opening in a long snout, the lower jaw does hinge, and there is a definite snap action of closure, yet the suck-in-draught still predominates. Even tubifex worms cannot be taken whole, if they are long. Small, sifted live daphnia is ideal (anything too fast would elude this quaint fish) as are pre-mashed morsels of prepared foods, e.g. shrimp, roe, prawn, porridge, finely chopped worms and meat, etc.

About the length and thickness of a commercial pipe cleaner, its body twists and bends according to the mood. A few short jabs of acceleration, a swim with a wavy undulation of the dorsal, otherwise the fish tends to be static, with the occasional slowly unwinding movement. Clearly it needs twigs to perch on, tall, reed-like plants to house in; streaky, murky light; mud-like silt base; clear of decaying vegetation and leaves but furnished with tubes, hollows, clumped twigs, flower pots, etc. DH 8–10, ph 7.2, 74°–80°F.

Usually only 3–5 in. long and 1⅛ in. thick, red brown in colour, overlaid with filigree pattern and a pale undercarriage, a long snout mouth. The male has a long thin red line, his body is wider due to the long row of skin folds in his undercarriage where the eggs are hatched.

It is the male who carries and hatches the eggs.

Spawning is done in top waters, and needs to be induced by multi-twigged areas in murky light interspersed with mildly lit clear waters. Cleanliness is appreciated; sterilization is overdoing it.

Spawning time darkens and brings out the male colours and patterns as he swims above, ahead, around and finally alongside the female, who is enticed to deposit the eggs in his brood pouch with an intense quivering of the rear part of her body. Repeated actions until the female is spent and the male pouch is full. Part adhesive at first, the eggs lose this as they mature. Care has to be taken as eggs falling out of the male pouch seldom hatch.

At 80°F. they usually hatch in 36–48 hours, and are free swimming in a week. Jerky spasms mark their movements, rather than rhythmic undulations.

A welcome newcomer to the popular fish tank range.


PLATIES. (Also Swordtails and Mollies). One of the most loved of the live bearers; tough, pretty and adaptable they will spawn anywhere laying not eggs but giving birth direct to fully formed baby fish, anything up to several dozens at a time. Seldom does an aquarist forget the first spawning, usually totally unexpected by him, when the graceful shoal of minute babies suddenly are there; jerky swimmers for a few hours, and then beautiful little fish. Rapidly they grow, rapidly they colour, and rapidly you learn (alas!) to cease repeating the wonderful story to your friends – because they had already heard similar and equally wondrous news from other aquarists! Nevertheless it really is a great thrill.

In the old days we had neat divisions, and separate names, for the red platy, the blue, the white, the yellow, the gold, the speckled, the wagtail, the high-fin, the tuxedo, the Berlin, and so on. We still try and keep up with the flood of beautiful new strains that line breeding has fixed, but the very genus now has got so inter-bred as to be scientifically 'no longer valid'. Paricularly has this been accentuated by cross breeding with Swordtails and with Mollies, two other famous line bearers, and the Swords are also no longer valid!

The main Swordtails used to be green or red; then came a stream of variations of which the modern favourites are High-fin and Lyre tail types and combinations. Fantastically beautiful fish, especially the males with their long trailing elongation of the lower part of the tail fin, earning the name of Swordtail.

So, too, with the velvet black Molly, the speckled, the green, the Lyre tail, the sail fin, the high fin – to name a few.

All the live bearers can easily be sexed; the female anal fin (near the vent) is short and round, the male one is long and pointed being used as a gonopodium for physical fertilisation. In addition, the male tail fin is distinctly thicker and more pointed in the lowest part; a characteristic shown in the extreme by the Swordtail.

So inter-bred, in so many waters, at so many temperatures and conditions that almost any reasonable tank will do. The females go on to spawn more than once after only one fertilisation, and regularly do so in a community tank. After all, the difficult part of 'hatching eggs' has already been taken care of inside the female; the future young being folded in two, all the heads pointed towards the same focal spot which accordingly swells and darkens as the heads and eyes develop, and is known as the 'gravid spot'. When intense in colour, the spawning is near.

Gestation varies, especially with the nervous Mollies whose high-strung nerves demand privacy, but a spring, summer, autumn rhythm is 'natural'. Greedy Man often forces throughout the year spawnings every few weeks till the wrecked and exhausted female is spent. Excessive inbreeding ought to be avoided by the infusion of new stock.

Gregarious and peaceful, these fish have all long since learnt to live with anyone anywhere. Jealousy, though, is still a characteristic and two males with only one female is asking for trouble; a breeding trio of one male plus two females is usual.

Not unknown, is a change of sex – almost always from female to male. At a sort of half-way stage in this transition the process has been known to slow down or stop, resulting in a particularly ill-tempered fish.

PLECOSTOMUS. (Sucking Catfish). Amazon. 8 in. Firmly established as a favourite; it works hard cleaning up the tank, minds its own business, and is quaint to look at.

The drab markings clearly show that it prefers gloom to glare; shady nooks under rock ledges, between crevices, below overhangs, all suit it best. Often such characteristics are associated with muddy waters, but such would be fatal for this fish which gives an unmistakable clue to those who will look : its huge, sucker mouth not only enables it to grip on to ledges, although it prefers not to stick upside down but to hang tail-down, but also to resist strong water currents. Hence it likes free-flowing waters rich in oxygen; aeration is particularly helpful. A second clue is the enormous appetite it has for algae; found in clear swift waters, strongly-lit. Hence this fish needs a hiding place, well sheltered from the light, during the day; emerging at dawn and dusk to work and clean and remove algae.

Its small eyes, sub-terminal snout (rather than the vast suction-type mouth) indicate a rummaging in the bottom half among nooks and crannies, rather than an open swimmer. So, too, of course do the strongly-arched back and the flat belly. Obviously a dark base would help, sand being preferred or dirt or mud.

Again such conditions, like swift waters, seldom go with great heat so that 68°–77°F. is ideal; ph 7.0, DH 8–12.

All its aspects suggest flight rather than fight; and, in fact, it can accelerate away very fast for short bursts from dangers; then hanging motionless and merged in with the surroundings, hoping to remain unnoticed. A certain restlessness accompanies this ability for limited swims so that the fish tends to be a wanderer, ranging fairly extensively in its search for food. But, emphatically, it is not a scavenger, indifferent to dirt; rather, it tends to be fastidious, with a strong preference for clean green algae.

Wild specimens have been known to reach 17 in. lengths, but the usual aquarium ones are 5–8in.

OTHER SUCKING CATFISH have long been kept in the aquarium, with the same basic preferences and characteristics as above described. The small Ottocinclus types, rarely growing more than 3 in., and liked just because of that; the medium sized Aymonieri from Siam, and the relatively new Myersi from China (which can survive in really cool temperatures of only 65°F.). Between them these types can satisfy the demands of most aquarists.

Then, too, are the droll but lovable, 'upside down' swimmers like the Synodontis from Africa, with their long whiskers. Of these the Congo variety, S. Nigriventris, has the added advantage of not growing too large, usually less than 3 in., and of being able to withstand much higher temperatures than the others e.g. up to 80°F. in comfort.

ORDINARY CATFISH are not being here detailed, because this has already been done in earlier books by me. They are extremely well known, are a 'must' for every tank, and, unlike their cousins described above, are not over sensitive to dirt. Yet even they take a dim view of a tank base wholly covered with mulm.

Basically their demands are the same, though less enthusiastic vegetarians they will eat tubifex worms and meat scraps quite eagerly. Bottom dwellers, it's the bottom one single inch of tank conditions and temperatures that affect them most; many aquarists tend to be careless about that particular vital one inch. At least thirty varieties are normally available of these peaceful, gregarious hard-workers.

SCATS (Scatophagus argus). 6 in. East Pacific Coast. One of those mobile fish that go anywhere, with anybody and whom you meet wherever you go. Basically they are sea-water, ocean shore, scavengers who get carried away by their enthusiastic appetites right up the deltas, creeks and estuaries into inland brackish, and even fresh waters. Extensively found along the vast Pacific coast line they are an established aquarium favourite. Newly caught, brackish water specimens need to be slowly acclimatized to fresh water – but not to acid water – and the aquarist should beware of these 'very cheap' ones. Otherwise they are resilient, peaceful although a shade greedy with an ever-empty stomach.

Many varieties are known like the red tiger, or the green, or the yellow but the fish tend to change both colour and even markings according to mood and condition. Provided the water is not actually acid, they can survive almost anything, and will eat algae as readily as flesh foods, worms or daphnia.

The slightly uncouth mouth, the rather untidy hotch-potch of dots and flashes, is in keeping with their scavenger characteristics. Totally lacking pride or in fierceness, they will not attack, rather they are timid and will scamper off, and are, therefore, happiest in the safety of shoals. Established shoals tend to be unruly, darting hither and thither, calling to each other, restlessly searching, always

on the go; exhilarating or wearying to others! Their
laterally compressed bodies show an obvious preference
for crevices or reed-like thickets, and their round circular
bodies indicate that water depths of 12–24 in. are better
than shallows. Their changing colours show their adapta-
bility to bright clear waters, free flowing; to heavy over-
growths, and even to mud, provided the waters flow and
do not get stagnant, an important point too often overlooked.

Aeration, and a salt bath will usually tone them up. The
more hunch backed the fish, the older it is. A safe hiding
place is a 'must' for lonely specimens who will rush out to
grab food and then tear back to safety again. DH 10–12,
ph 7.4, 75°–82°F. all suit them.

SPINY EELS. (Mastocembelus argus). Siam. 8 in. Obviously
keen on burrowing into the sand base, which should not
be sharp or scratchy, therefore, the long thin body, the
deep protected eyes, and the sub-terminal mouth all indicate that. Yet, the mouth shows more: it is part
aggressive, part scavenger; in fact, it has teeth. Hence the
fish likes tubifex worms and is not at all interested in green
stuffs; in fact, it is allergic to green water.

Like its cousin the Plecostumus, just described, it requires
the same clear, clean fast-flowing waters, dim light, nooks
and crannies of rocks, twigs or tree bark. Also it prefers a
soft base, mud rather than mulm where it hunts hidden or
buried flesh foods, ignoring the green plants. As a
scavenger to burrow into, under and through the sand –
it's unbeatable.

The small mouth makes it safe to keep in a community
tank. So too are the many similar spiny eels like the
West African M. Loennbergi or the Indian M. Pancalus.

Spawning is relatively easy, provided the aquarist follows
the clues shown by the heightened breeding colours; from

being drab, bottom dwellers, buried by day, they suddenly change: intense colours, and frantic day movements. This total reversal clearly explains their insistent demand for strong, twiggy, long-thick-root-like tangles just below the water surface. Without these they seldom spawn readily. DH 10, ph 7.0, 75°–80°F. also help, as does a little-distant, but yet strong, top lighting penetrating through the tangled clumps for an hour or so before the event. The adhesive eggs are hidden in the tangles, hatch in 48–72 hours; the jerky fry staying hidden at water surface become free swimming in a week or so. A sure sign of healthy growth is when the inch long fry begin visiting the tank base, finally to desert the surface tangles altogether in a month when the snout has developed. At the age of three months the total length may still be under three inches. Aeration helps hatching and growth, as does dim streaky light once the eggs are laid.

Catching the adults is difficult, partly because they can accelerate rapidly, and twist and turn like a Grand Prix Car Racer, and partly because they can be almost invisible, completely buried in the sand with only the snout tip breathing surface. A planting stick run carefully an inch below sand level dislodges them. It can be done very gently because these quaint fish are responsive and tameable. If you win their confidence they will swim into, and curl into almost any tempting net or cup-like 'home' within six or so inches of tank base; obviously playing and showing off for you.

ZEBRA. (Brachydanio rerio). India. 2½ in. Another firm favourite right from the very early days. Graceful torpedo body, balanced and slim, nicely finned; obviously a very fast swimmer, with great manouvreability and energy. Add the beautifully clear cut longitudinal stripes, entirely free of smudges, and a sheening body – obviously we have a fish that loves open clean bright waters, free flowing if possible, with ample room to swim and play. Its bright clear eyes and medium mouth, slightly super terminal; its general friendly appearance, lacking in pugnacity, denote its love of companionship, its ability to stay in shoals, to laugh and to frolic in mid-to-top waters.

Coming from India where temperatures fluctuate between slight frost in winter and intense heat in summer, it has a wide temperature tolerance. Its barbels, together with its bubbling energy, denote a healthy appetite; its extreme mobility is also not out of place with its short, but gay life span of three years or so.

A prolific breeder, the parents eat the free-scattered eggs with relish unless prevented by a false bottom, rough pebble base with ample crevices to trap the eggs, or some other such provision. Spawning often lasts a week or more, giving 100 to 150 eggs per day; hatching in 36–48 hours at 75°F. they become free swimming in two days. Tangles of roots, or of twigs, just below water surface and strong overhead lighting are conducive to spawning. DH 8–12, ph 7.0 to 7.5, 75°–78°F. would also help. Plenty of foods are essential, flesh rather than vegetable, though both are taken.

Many are the variations:

B. *Albolineatus* (the Pearl Danio), just as hardy and just as playful.

B. *Nigrofasciatus* (Spotted Danio), with a lovely delicate mouth; less pushing, more gentle, and smaller (only $1\frac{3}{4}$) this Indo-Chinese dweller tends to be overshadowed by its more boisterous cousins. It prefers slightly higher temperatures of 74°–80°F., and particularly appreciates cleanliness.

B. *Malabaricus* (Giant Danio), considerably more able to 'take care of itself' and growing to six inches or more it clearly wants large free waters and would be too much for small fish; otherwise peaceful and gregarious.

# CHAPTER SEVENTEEN

# USEFUL FACTS

If your heating fails don't pour in hot water and risk cracking the glass. Fill a clean tall bottle (no smell please!) e.g. a milk bottle with very hot water and stand it in the tank with its mouth protruding above water surface. The heat from the milk bottle should maintain the temperature all night, especially if you cover the whole tank with a rug.

*Proportion of litres to imperial gallons*
1 litre = 1,000 cubic centimetres = 1.7598 pints.
1 cubic foot = 28.31 litres.
1 pint = 0.5679 litres.
1 Imperial gallon = 4.5459 litres = 0.1605 cubic feet.
1 United States gallon = 3.785 litres = 0.1339 cubic feet.

*Weights*
1 kilogram = 1,000 grams = 1,00,000 milligrams = weight of one litre of water.
1 grain = 0.065 gramme.
15.432 grains = 1 gramme.

*Medicine Dip*
If you plan to give a sick fish a medicine bath for a few seconds or minutes; get a suitable sized net, dip this and the fish in the solution, leaving it free to swim inside the net, and remove both after the measured time lapse.

*Catching Fish*
Use two nets. With the smaller one chase the fish into

the bigger one, which should then be pulled upwards, not forwards.

If time permits, sink the big net right into the water, well spread out, and directly under the main feeding area; tempt the fish over the net with food, and then pull net upwards.

### Syphon Tube

Do not buy a rubber tube that is too short or the out-coming water is sure to spill one day. Let the tubing be amply long enough to reach full down to the floor, and have enough spare to coil inside the bucket on the floor. Now you can safely concentrate your attention on the tank end of the tubing.

Rather than let water just rush out, squeeze the rubber/plastic tubing to slow and stop the water flow as you move the tank end from one collection of dirt to another, syphoning only the dirt, with the minimum of water.

### Introducing New Fish

Feed the others first, extra well on this one occasion; float the container with the new fish in the tank to equalise the two water temperatures, say for five or ten minutes, and then float out the newcomers in the back corner, while the others are eating at the front.

### If your fish die

Take it back in aquarium water for the dealer to do a post-mortem examination. Please do not bring it back dry, but freshly preserved in water. The sooner the better.

### Medicines

It is often better to build up to the full dose in two or three stages, spaced a few hours apart. Each tank water has a 'different composition' and may contain elements to cause unexpected reactions, resulting in a dose that is 'too strong'. Sensitivity and patience are most helpful.

### Live Daphnia

Sometimes this goes off, say on a hot day, and contains much debris or dead daphnia. Pour all into a clean jam jar. Within seconds the dead and the sediment will sink to the bottom, leaving you free to pour out the rest carefully. If too many live daphnia stay trapped in the sediment, the jar can be refilled with water, allowed to settle and the top poured off again.

### Temperature

If this seems to fluctuate unduly, is your thermometer too near the top? Is it too near the heat of the electric top lighting which can warm the top inch or two of the water?

### Replacing Fish

If you have had two for a long time and one dies, please think before your replace. Has the survivor grown too large for the replacement? If so, why not buy two, and lessen the chance of bullying.

### Breeding

Far better, if you have time and space, than buying a breeding pair is to get a number of young adults, allow them to grow and to pair off naturally.

### Peat

Cover the base of a non-toxic (important please) container with peat and leave it soaking in rainwater all the time, replacing as you use. Say one inch of peat to six inches depth of water. Dim light discourages algae, etc. When the peat sinks it is 'mature'; it, and the saturated water, are both excellent for fish.

The stock solution should be easy to maintain as the water gets saturated before the peat. Always keep plenty in hand, well before you need it; even two months!

If in a hurry, you can heat a peat plus six parts of water solution, even boil it. But this will be ultra strong, perhaps toxic, and should be very heavily diluted before use.

## When in doubt

Part change the water with new water of the same temperature; clean the filter, including the carbon; skim the water surface; increase aeration; and feed with live foods. Dim light may help.

# Index